Exeter Medieval English Texts & Studies

General Editor: M.J. Swanton

ALDRED'S MARGINALIA

EXPLANATORY COMMENTS IN
THE LINDISFARNE GOSPELS

by

W.J.P. BOYD

University of Exeter : 1975

First published in 1975 by
University of Exeter Press
Reed Hall, Streatham Drive
Exeter, EX4 4QR
UK
www.ex.ac.uk/uep/

Printed digitally since 2003

ISBN 0 85989 036 8

Printed and bound by CPI Group (UK) Ltd, Croydon, CR0 4YY

CONTENTS

For Jean, without whose patience, humour and loving encouragement, this essay would have been still-born.

ACKNOWLEDGEMENTS

To Professor A.S.C. Ross I owe especial thanks for first suggesting that I should provide a commentary on these glosses from the standpoint of the discipline of Christian Theology, and for his great patience in discussing many points of detail. I owe much to his continual encouragement to persevere with these studies over a number of years. My thanks are also due to Professor J.R. Porter of Exeter University and to Professor Raphael Loewe of University College, London for help with Hebrew and Aramaic words and for much constructive criticism, and Dr. Michael Swanton of the English Department of Exeter University has given generous editorial help. They have helped to eradicate many mistakes and faults, and such as remain are entirely my own. My thanks are also due to the staffs of the Inter-Library Loans department of Exeter University Library and to the Keeper of Printed Books and his staff of the Bodleian Library for generous assistance.

St. Kew, 1975

W.J.P. BOYD

ABBREVIATIONS

ANT = The Apocryphal New Testament (ed. M.R. James, 1924).

Brown = R.E., *The Gospel according to John*, 2 vols., 1971.

Catena Aurea compiled by S. Thomas Aquinas.

CCSL = Corpus Christianorum Series Latina, (Turnhout, 1953ff).

CLA = E.A. Lowe, *Codices Latini Antiquiores*, Oxford, 1934–63.

cm = central margin of *Codex Lind.*

CM = Commentariorum in Mattheum libri (e.g. Hieronymi).

CMk = Commentarius in Euangelium secundum Marcum

Cod. Lind. = Codex Lindisfarnensis

CSEL = Corpus Scriptorum Ecclesiasticorum Latinorum (Vienna, 1866ff).

DTC = Dictionnaire de Théologie Catholique (ed. A. Vacant *et al.*, in 15 vols., 1903–50).

ERE = Encyclopedia of Religion and Ethics (ed. J. Hastings, 12 vols., 1908–26).

Etym = Etymologiarum siue Originum Isidori (ed. W.M. Lindsay, 2 vols., Oxford, 1911).

EVV = English Versions of the Bible.

Exp. in Mt = Expositio in Matthaeum (Paschasii Radberti).

GCS = Die griechischen christlichen Schriftsteller der ersten drei Jahrhunderte (Leipzig, 1897–1941; Berlin & Leipzig 1953; Berlin, 1954ff).

Haddan & Stubbs = A.W. Haddan and W. Stubbs (eds.), *Councils and Ecclesiastical Documents relating to Great Britain and Ireland*, Oxford, 1869–71.

Hefele = C.J. Hefele, *A History of the Christian Councils from the original documents to the close of the Council of Nicaea*, Edinburgh, 1872–6.

Hefele-LeClercq = C.J. Hefele, *Histoire des Conciles d'après les documents originaux*, revised by R.P. Dom le Clercq, Paris, 1907–38.

hom in ev. = Homilia in Evangelium (Gregorii Magni).

lhm = left hand margin in *Cod. Lind.*

LXX = the Septuagint, the Greek version of the Old Testament.

Mansi = J.D. (ed.) *Sacrorum Conciliorum nova et amplissima collectio*, 31 vols., (Florence, 1759–98).

NEB = The New English Bible.

NT = New Testament.

OnS = Onomastica Sacra (ed. Paul De Lagarde, Hildesheim, 1966).

Op. impf. Mt = Opus imperfectum in Matthaeum (Pseudonymi Chrysostomi).

Abbreviations, continued

OT = Old Testament.

OW = Origenes Werke (for the works of Origen of Alexandria in *GCS*).

PG = *Patrologia Graeca* (ed. J.P. Migne, 168 vols., Paris, 1857–66).

PL = *Patrologia Latina* (ed. J.P. Migne, 221 vols., Paris, 1844–64).

rhm = right hand margin of *Cod. Lind.*

SDm = *De Sermone Domini in monte* (libros duos Augustini).

TLL = *Thesaurus Linguae Latinae.*

Tr = *In Iohannis Euangelium Tractatus* (Sancti Aurelii Augustini, in CCSL 36).

T.U. = *Texte und Untersuchungen zur Geschichte der altchristlichen Literatur,* begründet von O. von Gebhardt und A Harnack (Leipzig, 1882ff).

INTRODUCTION

One of the most treasured possessions of the British Museum, the manuscript of the Lindisfarne Gospels[1] is an outstanding example of Hiberno-Saxon book-production. This skill reached its zenith in Northumbria in the late seventh and eighth centuries. Its artistic inspiration arose from a coalescing of several kinds of artistic traditions from very different cultures, so that it was an art which transcended purely national or geographical boundaries. The Lindisfarne Gospels codex was only one of many such illuminated Gospel books. We may recall the so-called *Canterbury Gospels* (*CLA* II, 214), the *Book of Durrow* (*CLA* II, 273), the *Book of Mac Regol* (*CLA* II, 231), the *Book of Kells* (*CLA* II, 274), the *St Chad Gospels* (*Mt – L* 3,9) in Lichfield Cathedral (*CLA* II, 159), the Southern English *Codex Aureus*, now lodged in the Stockholm National Library (*CLA* XI, 1642), the *Eternach Gospels* (*CLA* V, 578 and VIII, 1215) and the *St Gall Gospels* (*CLA* VII, 901), as examples of this rich and widespread skill.[2] However, there is little doubt that of those manuscripts that have survived, the Lindisfarne Gospels codex is one of the noblest.

The Lindisfarne Gospel codex is written on 258 vellum leaves, which measure an average 25 cm wide x 34.5 cm long. The codex opens with an ornamental 'carpet' page. It is a design of pure and varied colours out of which a cross emerges. There are five such carpet pages in the codex, each of different design and colour scheme. Originally there may have been six: one for each Gospel, one to start the codex, and possibly one to finish it. The five extant carpet pages are found on folios 2V, 26V, 94V, 138V and 210V. There are eight pages of decorated text at 3R, 8R, 19R, 27R, 29R, 95R, 139R and 211R; and sixteen pages of beautifully decorated, arcaded Eusebian canons (10R–17V). The Latin text is written in black ink, in double

1. British Library MS Cotton Nero DIV. The standard edition is that of W.W. Skeat, who took over the task of editing Anglo-Saxon versions of the Gospels begun by J.M. Kemble and C. Hardwick, whose edition of *St Matthew* appeared in 1858. Skeat continued their interrupted work and published *St Mark* in 1871, *St Luke* in 1874, *St John* in 1878; and then, because he disagreed with the editorial methods of his predecessors, he produced a new edition of *St Matthew* in 1887. His editions are known collectively as *The Holy Gospels in Anglo-Saxon, Northumbrian and Old Mercian Versions,* Cambridge, 1871–87. Skeat's version superseded that of J. Stevenson and G. Waring, published by the Surtees Society, vols. 28, 43, 48 (1854–65). Skeat's version is still useful as it supplies immediate comparisons with other Old English versions of the Gospels; but allowance must be made for occasional errors in palaeography, and the dated character of some of the critical opinions expressed. The chief convenience of his edition is in presenting the Latin text and its accompanying Old English gloss in easily legible form. A definitive facsimile edition exists: *Evangeliorum Quattuor Codex Lindisfarnensis,* ed. T.D. Kendrick, *et al,* Oltun et Lausanna, 1956–60.

2. Cf. E.A. Lowe, *Codices Latini Antiquiores.* (*CLA*), Oxford, 1934–63. For the *Book of Durrow* see also the beautiful edition of A.A. Luce, *et al, Evangeliorum Quattuor Codex Durmachensis,* Oltun, Lausanna and Freiburg, 1960; for the *Book of Kells* see also the edition of E.H. Alton and P. Meyer, *Evangeliorum Quattuor Codex Cenannensis,* Berne, 1950–1; Edward Sullivan, *The Book of Kells,* London, 1914, and F. Henry, *Irish Art,* 2nd ed., London, 1965, pp. 159–202.

1

columns in a boldly-written half-uncial script of a typically Irish style of penmanship. There are four full-colour portraits of the Evangelists, each with his characteristic symbol (25V, 93V, 137V, 209V). The strong line-drawing points to the influence of Graeco-Roman naturalism; the incredibly intricate and varied designs of the decorative schemes used for the carpet pages and decorated text pages testify to the fertility of invention of Celtic abstraction; whilst the rich ornamentation of those same designs is eloquent testimony to the Anglo-Saxon genius for illumination. In between the lines of the Latin text and at times in the margins of the folios is an Anglo-Saxon gloss in the north Northumbrian dialect, written by a priest who tells us in the colophon to the codex that his name is 'Aldred, the son of Alfred and of a worthy woman' (alfredi natus aldredus uocor: bonae mulieris/.i. tilw', filius eximius loquor). Aldred's gloss was written much later than the original manuscript, and both the Gospel codex and its accompanying Anglo-Saxon gloss reflect the cultural history of the community in which they were produced.

Gospel codices were never produced in a vacuum. They were always the production of a community rich enough to afford the gift of sheep from which the necessary vellum could be obtained. As the name of the Lindisfarne Gospels suggests, the codex was produced in the monastery on the island of Lindisfarne, just off the northeast coast of England. Access is governed by the sea and its tides. Bede's description of the island is as true to-day as it was in his own time: 'The isle of Lindisfarne ... which place as the tide ebbs and flows, is twice a day encircled by the sea's waves like an island; and again, twice, when the beach is left dry, becomes contiguous with the land'.[3] To-day the modern pilgrim can cross at low tide by a convenient tarmac causeway: in Bede's day access at low tide was on foot across the wet sands. If the worldly minded could ride on horseback, for the monks of Lindisfarne to travel on foot was regarded as obligatory and an integral part of their calling. We may note how in his biography of St Cuthbert, who was Lindisfarne's most famous bishop, Bede feels it is necessary to apologise for the fact that when a heavenly messenger visited the saint to relieve him of his suffering when he was ill, he arrived on horseback![4]

There is nothing very beautiful about this desolate isle with its unremarkable terrain, yet it was chosen by St Aidan (*d.* 651) when he was sent by his superiors at the monastery of Iona, in answer to a request of Oswald, king of Northumbria (633–41), for 'a bishop by whose instruction and ministry, the English nation which he governed, might learn the privileges of faith in our Lord and receive the sacraments'.[5] The Celtic missionaries were drawn to such remote sites because their isolation was

3. Cf. B. Colgrave and R.A.B. Mynors, *Bede's Ecclesiastical History of the English People,* Oxford, 1969, pp.218ff.
4. Cf. *Bedae vita sancti Cuthberti,* ed. B. Colgrave, *Two Lives of St Cuthbert,* Cambridge 1940, p.160.
5. Cf. Bede, *HE* III, 3; *op. cit.* in n.3, p.218.

conducive to good discipline and the uninterrupted life style of work and prayer (*laborare et orare*); furthermore, their relative inaccessibility made them a safe retreat from the hostility of unconverted pagan raiders. Monastic life at Lindisfarne continued peacefully enough, until the crisis in the inner life of the Church of Northumbria, caused by the tension between Roman and Celtic understandings of the faith, came to a head at the Synod of Whitby in 664. There the chosen champion of Celtic traditions was Bishop Colman of Lindisfarne. The eventual decisions of the Synod involved him in a crisis of conscience, and since his advice was ignored in favour of that of Abbot Wilfrid, the champion of the Roman Church, Colman withdrew from Lindisfarne, taking with him many Celtic and British monks.[6] A serious situation was thus created for the Northumbrian Church, since Lindisfarne was the centre of diocesan life. But energetic steps were taken to meet the crisis. Tuda was appointed Bishop of Lindisfarne; and even more importantly, Abbot Eata was summoned from Melrose Abbey to take charge of the monastery on the island. He asked his prior, Cuthbert, to accompany him. The two men came to Lindisfarne in 664, and set about introducing the still-controversial Roman Church traditions. In due course Cuthbert assumed full responsibility for the administration and spiritual oversight of the monastery. At first he met with considerable resistance from the monks, but gradually he won them over to a fanatical devotion to his leadership. Cuthbert was destined to become Lindisfarne's most famous bishop and saint. The cult of the saint began during his own lifetime and spread rapidly after his death in 687.

Now it was the desire to honour St Cuthbert that led his successor, Bishop Eadbert, to commission the production of the Lindisfarne Gospels codex. Eadbert died in 698 and was succeeded in turn by Bishop Eadfrith, who ruled Lindisfarne until his death in 721. Aldred in his famous colophon to the Gospel codex tells us that it was Eadfrith who wrote the Latin text of the codex: + Eadfrið biscop (*alt. to* biscob) lindisfearnensis æcclesiæ / he ðis boc aurát æt fruma gode 7 sc'e / cuðberhte (259Rb). It has been thought that Eadfrith would have been in all probability too busy with episcopal duties to undertake the vast work of writing and illuminating the manuscript once he had been consecrated bishop, so that the **favoured conjectural date** for the completion of the MS is *c.* 698. It has been estimated that the codex would have taken at least two years to finish, so that the work must have been put in hand well within Eadbert's episcopate. Eadfrith was succeeded by Ethelwald, who, because of his great skill as a craftsman and artist, was able to enrich the monastery with many gifts. He provided the codex with a stout cover of gold and jewels — 'as well he knew how' (sua he uel cuðæ), comments Aldred in the colophon. Ethelwald was assisted in the metalwork by Billfrith, the anchorite, who, as Alfred tells us, 'forged the ornaments which are on the outside of it and adorned it with

6. Cf. Bede, *HE* III, 26; *op. cit.* in n.3, pp.308f.

gold and gems and also with gilded silver — pure metal' (he gismioðade ða ,' gihríno ða ðe útan ón sint 7 hit gi- / hrínade mið golde 7 mið gimmum æc / mið su^ulfre of' gylded faconleas feh). Aldred then tells us of his own connection with the great Gospel codex: 'And Aldred, unworthy and most miserable priest, glossed it in English between the lines with the help of God and St Cuthbert. And by means of the three 'sections' he made a home for himself — the section of Matthew was for God and St Cuthbert, the section of Mark was for the bishop, the section of Luke for the members of the Community ... and the section of St John was for himself (*explanatory note*: for his soul) ... so that through the grace of God he may gain acceptance into Heaven; happiness and peace, and through the merits of St Cuthbert, advancement and honour, wisdom and sagacity on earth. Eadfrith, Ethelwald, Billfrith, Aldred made, or, as the case may be, embellished this Gospel-book for God and St Cuthbert.'[7]

What Aldred does not tell us is that in fact he lived and worked over two hundred years later than Billfrith. However we may note in passing how completely he had identified with the illustrious tradition of scholarship and art that he inherited as a member of the community, so that he can add his own name to that of his pre-decessors without any sense of incongruity. The interval between Billfrith and Aldred for the history of the community held many stormy events. In 793 the island of Lindisfarne sustained its first severe raid at the hands of the Danes.[8] Some monks managed to escape and when the Danes withdrew, they returned to their ruined homes and church and manfully began the work of restoration. Lindisfarne escaped further molestation until in 875 Viking armies once more threatened their island refuge. The monks then decided to evacuate completely, and Bishop Eardulf with Abbot Eadred led the community into exile. They took with them the relics of St Cuthbert, and of other holy men, and together with their precious Gospel codex, they set out on a quest for a new and safe retreat.[9] The quest was to last for about seven years. Then, after the death of Halfdene, the Danish chieftain who had wreaked such havoc in Northumbria and driven them from their island home of Lindisfarne, Abbot Eadred brought off a masterly coup. He went to the Danish host and claimed that his own master, none other than St Cuthbert himself, had appeared to him in a vision and instructed him to make the young Danish prince Guthred their

7.   The colophon continues: 7 aldred p'sb'r indignus 7 misserrim' / mið godes fultu'mæ 7 sc'i cuðberhtes / hit of' glóesade ón englisc. 7 hine gihamadi / mið ðæm ðríim dælu'. Matheus dæl / gode 7 sc'e cuðberhti. Marc dæl / ðæm bisc'. 7 lucas dæl ðæm hiorode / ... 7 sc'i ioh' dæl f'hine (f'e hissaule) seolfne þte... þ te he/hæbbe ondfong ðerh godes milsæ on heofnu'. / séel 7 sibb on eorðo forðgeong 7 giðyngo / uisdóm 7 snyttro ðerh sc'i cuðberhtes earnunga. / + Eadfrið. oeðiluald. billfrið. aldred. / hoc euange' d'o 7 cuðberhto construxer't ⱶ ornauerunt. (259Rb).

8.   Cf. *The Anglo-Saxon Chronicle* transl. by G.N. Garmonsway, London, 1954, p.57.

9.   Cf. T. Arnold, etc., *Symeonis Monachi Opera Omnia,* London, 1882–5, Rolls Series 75, I, pp.56–8, 61–9, 207; II, p.110.

new leader. At a signal Bishop Eardulf led the young prince Guthred into view on the brow of a hill, and the Danish host simultaneously and enthusiastically acclaimed him as their new leader. Guthred rewarded the churchmen with a gift of land which included Chester-le-Street, where the community settled from 883 until 995, when it finally moved to its new cathedral home in Durham.[10] Aldred joined the community about 960. He worked in the scriptorium with a team of other scribes.[11] His context is that of the vigorous reform of the monastic houses and the general revival of Church life and of learning in the reign of the West Saxon monarch Edgar (957–75), which we have come to know as 'the Benedictine Rennaissance'. In addition to his work on the Lindisfarne Gospels Aldred also extended and glossed most of the Durham Ritual,[11] as well as adding a partial, interlinear and unsigned Latin gloss to Bede's *Commentary on Proverbs*.[12] Aldred rose to be provost in the community by at least 970, which office was second in rank under the Bishop. We know nothing of his death.

Aldred's Lindisfarne Gospels gloss is virtually a word for word translation of the underlying Latin, which he followed with very great faithfulness. For example in *L* 12,6 instead of five sparrows being *sold* for two farthings, we have the misspelling, *ueniunt*, which he dutifully glossed by *cymeð* (come). He did not try to correct the text to the right reading *ueneunt*. At times he inverts the natural order of Anglo-Saxon words, as in *L* 4,6 where *die sabbati'* is glossed by *dæge sun'*; this is deliberate so that he can follow his text even more closely.[13] However, in some seventy explanatory notes, made usually in the margins of the text, and occasionally interlineally, Aldred is able to expand on his interpretations to some extent. He still keeps himself on a tight rein, as it were, but his comments are invaluable in illustrating the state of Gospel exegesis in Northumbria after a century of Danish expansion and resultant upheaval in the Church. Sometimes his own distinctive personal viewpoint on controversial questions of the day shines through with remarkable clarity. The study which follows represents a collection of all these marginal comments, with the exception of just one or two examples which have been already fully discussed elsewhere. Reference is made to such discussions at the appropriate point.

10. Cf. E. Craster, 'The Patrimony of St Cuthbert', *English Historical Review*, 69 (1954), 177–99.

11. See T.J. Brown *et al.*, ed., *The Durham Ritual*, Copenhagen, 1969; esp. pp. 15–28 for the palaeographical characteristics of Aldred's fellow scribes.

12. MS. Bodley 819. The glosses are attributable to Aldred on palaeographical grounds.

13. The character of Aldred's gloss has been widely discussed; cf. A.S.C. Ross, 'The Errors in the Old English Gloss to the Lindisfarne Gospels', *Review of English Studies*, 8, (1932), 385–94; and 'Notes on the method of glossing employed in the Lindisfarne Gospels', *Transactions of the Philological Society*, 1933, esp. 116–7 for inverted glosses.

ALDRED'S COMMENTARY

1 *Mt* 1, 6   (27Vb4–6*rhm*)

uriae / uᵘries wif (Uriah's wife) / ðæs cempa. hine geheht dauid of-
slaa f'e hire ðingu*m*. bersabe wæs hire noma. ðy wæs salomones
moder ðæs cyniges (Of the warrior. David ordered him to be
killed for her sake. Bersabe was her name. She was the mother of
Solomon the king).

The explanation is accurate. Uriah was an Israelite soldier who served under King
David. The king contrived Uriah's death in battle, so that it looked like a natural
casualty of war, and the way would then be clear for David to marry his widow,
Bathsheba. The gloss is based on the narrative in 2 *Sam* 11,2–12,25, one of the
famous tales of passion, conspiracy and divine exposure in the *OT*. The Latin name
form Bersabe, is not derived from the Vulgate, which in 2 *Sam* 11,3 has the form
Bethsabee, which is Jerome's attempt to transliterate the Hebrew name בת-שבע ,
bath-sheba', literally 'daughter of (the deity) Sheba'. The usual transliteration in the
EVV from the Hebrew is *Bathsheba*. Aldred gives us a name form which is derived
from the *LXX* name form βηρσαβεέ, no doubt mediated through an Old
Latin text, as he did not know Greek. Bathsheba was the mother of Solomon, who
was her second son by king David, her first child dying in early infancy.[14]

2 *Mt* 1,18 (beginning)[15]   (29R)

uute ᵒdlice suæ wæs cristes cneureso (thus indeed was Christ's
genealogy).

The marginal comment shows how Aldred interpreted the Latin text *CHRISTI
AUTEM GENERATIO SIC ERAT*. It could be interpreted as a summary conclusion
of the genealogy, and Aldred's comment shows that this is how he understood the
sentence; or it could refer to the birth narrative which immediately follows, and this
is how the *EVV* usually translate the underlying Greek: 'This is the story of the birth
of the Messiah' (*NEB*). Possibly it was the ambiguity in the original text, which led
to the variant reading γέννησις (attested by MSS K L Π ˋand Origen) for the
original γένεσις (attested by MSS p¹ א B C P W), which normally denotes
'origin' and so could logically include both the genealogy as well as the birth

14. Cf. 2 *Sam* 12,24; 1 *Kg* 1, 11–17; 2,13; 1 *Chron* 3,5.
15. *Mt* 1,18 (29R) is an elaborate ornamental text page. The gloss occurs at the top left hand
side of the page and is tucked in under the top left cross stroke of the capital letter X (Chi).
The first three Greek letters of the name of Christ (XPI) form the main architecture for the
illuminated decorative scheme.

narrative in its scope. The variant reading γέννησις, 'birth', anticipates the immediately ensuing birth narrative, and so looks like a scribal emendation intended to resolve the ambiguity inherent in the original reading.[16]

The Fathers bear witness to the division of interpretation, so Pseudo-Chrysostom writes, 'so that nobody who heard should suppose that the birth was like that of any of the preceding Fathers (*Mt* 1,1–17), he abruptly breaks off the thread of his narrative ... as if to say ... "but Christ's birth was not this kind, but as follows. In what manner? Mary, when she was betrothed to Joseph, before they came together..." '.[17] He then emphasizes how the virgin birth made Christ's birth unique. However, such a view was theologically difficult, for it threatened belief in the true humanity of Christ, and posed the implicit question as to why the evangelist had bothered to include the genealogy at all, if it was beside the point. The pendulum of opinion swung back almost naturally, so Remigius of Auxerre (*c.* 841–908) could say, 'Yet it might be referred to what preceded it in this way: the generation of Christ was as I have described it thus, "Abraham begat Isaac" ...'[18] Rabanus Maurus (776 or 784–856) frankly admits that the sentence is capable of a double exegesis,[19] and attempts a synthesis by explaining the genealogy as an account of Christ's birth as Son of Man, whereas the virgin birth witnesses to his birth as Son of God. What helped this eirenic synthesis were the interpretations which the Church writers placed upon the symbols for the four canonical Gospels: the lion for Mark, the ox for Luke, the flying eagle for John and the human figure of a man for Matthew. These Gospel symbols are, of course, pre-Christian in origin; for example, they once represented the four chief deities of Assyrian religion: Nergal (the winged lion), Marduk (the winged bull), Nebo (the man), Ninib (the eagle). The prophet Ezekiel introduced them into Hebraic thought: cf. *Ezek* 1,4–13; 10,14, where the four creatures who surrounded the Almighty each had four faces representing the four symbols. This was an ingenious device as it meant that the creatures could move in any of the four directions of the compass without turning. The symbolism entered Christian iconography through the influence of apocalyptic. In the Apocalypse these four creatures stand continually before the throne of the Almighty; but now each beast has only one face which differentiates it from its companions *(Rev* 4,6–8). With the decline of apocalyptic, the symbols became transferred to the four-fold canon of the Gospels, though not without some preliminary argument as to which symbol belonged to which Gospel.

16. Cf. G.D. Kilpatrick, *The Origins of the Gospel according to St Matthew*, Oxford, 1946, p.52.

17. Pseudo-Chrysostomus (of uncertain date), *Opus imperfectum in Matthaeum*, Homilia 1, *PG* 56,630.

18. Cited by St Thomas Aquinas, *Catena Aurea in quattuor Evangelia*, ed. P.A. Guarienti, Marietti, 1953.

19. *Commentariorum in Matthaeum libri octo*, 1.3: *Haec sententia bifarie poni potest* (*PL* 107, 747D). Cf. also Paschasius Radbertus, *Expositio in Matthaeum*, his *Praefatio* and comment on *Mt* 1,18 (*PL* 120,37–45; 100C–102A).

St Augustine of Hippo (354–430) wanted to attach the lion to Matthew's Gospel;[20] but his argument did not prevail. By Aldred's time, of course, the connections of the symbols with their respective Gospels were firmly established and invariable. When the Fathers came to adduce reasons as to why an individual Gospel should have a particular symbol attached to it, the stock reason given for assigning the man to Matthew was the genealogy. St Jerome (*c.* 342–420) in his commentary on Ezekiel sees the opening words of St Matthew as a clear assertion of the humanity of Christ.[21] When Aldred came to interpret *GENERATIO* in *Mt* 1,18 he would doubtless observe that the word was first used at *Mt* 1,1 to introduce the genealogy, and he would be powerfully reminded of this tradition every time he worked on the Lindisfarne Gospel codex and saw the four illuminated portraits of the Evangelists, each with his symbol and the title of the symbol.[22] All this would help to swing the balance of opinion in his own mind towards the genealogy rather than exclusively towards the birth narrative.

3 *Mt* 1,18 (29R)

MATER / moder (mother) / to gemanne nalles to habbanne f' wif
(to take care of, by no means to have as a wife).

Skeat should have connected this marginal comment with *DESPONSATA* which renders μνηστευθείσης 'betrothed'. Aldred supplies four glosses for *DESPONSATA*: *biwoedded* (betrothed), ⊥ *beboden* (commended, or, committed), ⊥ *befeastnad* (or entrusted to, commended to) ⊥ *betaht* (entrusted to, committed to). Of these four, the first gloss is a correct translation, and the remainder reveal the point of the marginal explanation, namely that Aldred is reproducing apocryphal Gospel tradition on the life of the Virgin Mary. As this tradition also governs the next explanatory comment, it will be convenient to discuss them together.

---

20. *De Consensu Evangelistarum* I, 6 (*CSEL* 43,p.9f) where he argues that the lion as a symbol of royal dignity ought to denote the first Gospel which portrays the royal dignity of the Son of God most clearly. See F.C. Grant, *The Gospels: their origin and growth*, London, 1957, pp.65ff for a discussion of the Gospel symbols.

21. *Commentariorum in Hiezechielem Libri XV*, I,1,5–8: *Quidam quattuor evangelia, quos nos quoque in proemio Commentariorum Matthaei secuti sumus, horum animalium putant nominibus designari : Matthaei, quod quasi hominem descripserit: 'Liber generationis Iesu Christi filii Dauid, filii Abraham', leonis ad Marcum referunt: 'Initium evangelii Iesu Christi filii Dei' ... vituli ad Lucae evangelium, quod a Zachariae incipit sacerdotio; aquilae ad Ioannis exordium...* (*CCSL* 75, p.11/191–200). Jerome refers to the preface to his commentary on St Matthew where he wrote: *Prima hominis facies Matheum significat qui quasi de homine exorsus est scribere: 'Liber generationis Iesu Christi, filii Dauid, filii Abraham'* (*CCSL* 77, p.3/59–60).

22. Cf. *Cod. Lind.* 25V, where the portrait of St Matthew bears the symbol of the man with the title *imago hominis*. The clean-shaven head with a halo, and a pair of wings, and the trumpet of the Gospel proclamation applied to his lips is seen just above the large halo of the evangelist.

4 *Mt* 1,18 (29R *rhm*)

Ioseph (unglossed) / abiathar ðe aldormon wæs in ðæm tíd in hierusalem. forebiscob. he bebeod maria iosephe to gemenne 7 to begeonganne (*a.f.* begoeonganne) mið claennisse (Abiathar the leader (?) was at that time High Priest in Jerusalem. He entrusted Mary to Joseph to take care of, and to deal with in purity).

The name Abiathar belongs to the apocryphal Gospel tradition found only in Pseudo-Matthew; for, as a matter of fact, there was no High Priest in Jerusalem of that name from the first High Priest Joshua, appointed in the sixth century BC until Matthias ben Theophilus, the last of the genuine High Priests in 67 AD.[23] In the *Gospel of Pseudo-Matthew* we have a fictitious biography of the Virgin Mary. A brief review of the relevant sections of Pseudo-Matthew will help to characterize the context within which Aldred's glosses and explanations gain their significance. The story there runs as follows: Mary's parents for a long time after their marriage had been childless, but they had not ceased to pray for a child. In answer to their prayer, an angel was sent to announce the miraculous conception of Mary to Joachim her father: 'Know that Anna has conceived a daughter of thy seed ... She will be in the temple of God and the Holy Spirit will abide in her ...'[24] When Mary was three years old, her parents took her to the temple in Jerusalem where she was placed in the charge of a community of virgins. When she was of a marriageable age, the priest Abiathar wished to obtain her as a wife for his son,[25] but Mary cut short these negotiations by announcing that she had sworn a vow of perpetual virginity; so a Council of Israel met in the temple to decide how best to help Mary carry out her vow, and to ascertain into whose keeping she should be entrusted.[26] The divine choice was Joseph, so *the High Priest Abiathar* solemnly entrusted her into his care.[27] Joseph was at first very dubious about accepting such a weighty charge, but was prevailed upon and so accepted Mary, provided that she had an escort of five more virgins to be her companions.[28] The virgins cast lots for a purple veil, and the lot

---

23. See F.W. Farrar, *The Herods*, London, 1899, pp.225–6 for a list of all the High Priests appointed in Jerusalem.

24. C. de Tischendorf, ed., *Evangelia Apocrypha*, Lipsiae, 1876, p.58.

25. *Tunc Abiathar sacerdos obtulit munera infinita pontificibus, ut acciperet eam filio suo tradendam uxorem. Prohibebat autem eos Maria dicens: 'Non potest fieri ut ego virum cognoscam aut me vir cognoscat'* (*Ibid*, p.65).

26. *Cum autem universus populus convenisset, surrexit Abiathar pontifex ... et ... dixit ... A sola vero Maria novus ordo placendi deo inventus est, quae promittit deo se virginem permanere. Unde mihi videtur ut per interrogationem nostram et responsionem dei possimus agnoscere cui debeat custodienda committi* (*Ibid*, pp.66–7).

27. *voce magna clamavit ad eum* (sc *Ioseph*) *Abiathar pontifex dicens: 'Veni et accipe virgam tuam...'* (*Ibid*, p.68).

28. *Tunc Ioseph accepit Mariam cum aliis quinque virginibus, quae essent cum ea in domo Ioseph* (*Ibid*, p.70).

fell to Mary. When they joked that she had won the veil because she was 'the queen of virgins', an angel intervened to assert that it was not a joke, as that was precisely what her true status was.[29]

This apocryphal tradition that Mary was kept pure and chaste in the temple and entrusted to Joseph to guard in purity was widespread. We find a reference to it in Pseudo-Augustine, who explains that Joseph being a just man was rightly troubled when he discovered his betrothed was with child, for he had received her from none other source than the temple of the Lord, and was innocent of sexual relationship with her.[30] The gloss *to begeonganne mið claennisse,* is, therefore, embedded in this tradition, which in *Pseudo-Matthew* takes the form of a story of a trial by ordeal to prove the innocence of both Joseph and Mary. Happily the trial proves them to be both innocent of breaking a holy and sacred trust, and so becomes the occasion of general rejoicing at what is clearly understood to be a divinely created pregnancy.[31] All the probabilities are that Aldred knew this apocryphal tradition through *Pseudo-Matthew*, which was produced in either the eighth or ninth century to further the veneration of Mary as the 'Queen of Virgins'. The popularity of the tradition led to many recensions of the Latin text of this apocryphal Gospel, as part of the process of its wide dissemination.[32]

5 *Mt* 1,22   (29Vb 7cm)

propheta' / ðone witgo (the prophet) / in esaia

Aldred correctly identifies the quotation in *Mt* 1,23 as a composite quotation from Isaiah the prophet (cf. *Isa* 7,14; 8,8. 10 *LXX*).

6 *Mt* 5,3   (34Rb1 *rhm*)

Beati pauperes / eadge biðon ða ðorfendo (*a.f.* ðærfendo) (Blessed are the poor) / eadge biðon ða ðaerfe' þ is únspoedge menn ł unsynnige f'ðon hia agan godes ... (blessed are the poor, that is unwealthy or sinless men for they shall possess God's ...)

In an unfinished gloss, Aldred has correctly reproduced the usual way the Fathers understood the word 'poor' in this beatitude. In the *OT* the word 'poor' is represented by two words: עָנִי *'ani,* 'poor, lowly, oppressed', and אֶבְיוֹן *'ebhyôn,* 'poor, needy, oppressed'. Both words generally denote pious people who are not wealthy because they care more for obeying God's will than for amassing wealth, and who, out of their very devotion to the Law, often find themselves oppressed by

29. *Ibid.*
30. *Sermo* 195.4 (*PL* 39, 2108–9).
31. *Ps—Mt* 12.
32. For a full discussion of *Pseudo-Matthew* see E. Hennecke, *New Testament Apocrypha,* ed. W. Schneemelcher I, *Gospels and Related Writings,* London, 1963, pp.404–7.

the rich and the powerful ungodly.[33] Jerome expresses a view very similar to that of Aldred in content, if not in wording: 'the poor in spirit are those who embrace a voluntary poverty for the sake of the Holy Spirit'.[34] Aldred's explanation, then, is in line with the *OT* meaning of the word 'poor', and the patristic exegesis of this beatitude.

7 *Mt* 5,5 (34 Rb4−5 *rhm*)

terram / eorðo (earth) / f'ðon ða milde gbyes hlifgiendr(a) eorðo
(for the meek shall possess the land of the living).

Aldred may have derived the phrase ***hlifgiendra eorðo*** from the *OT* where the concept of the land of the living occurs at least fourteen times.[35] The Hebrew idiom אֶרֶץ חַיִּים *'erets ḥayyîm*, 'land of the living', normally denotes the present bustling world of men and affairs, albeit under the watchful sovereignty of God, as opposed to the kingdom of Sheol, the underworld of death.[36] However, in patristic exegesis the land of the living developed into a symbol of immortality, namely, the abode of blessed spirits; and this earth could be considered as the land of the living only in so far as the Kingdom of God was realized upon it. Pseudo-Chrysostom writes, 'This earth, however, as some say, as long as it is in its present state, is the land of the dead, because it is subject to vanity; when, on the other hand, it shall be freed from the slavery of corruption into the glorious freedom of the sons of God (*Rom* 8, 19−22) it becomes the land of the living, that the immortal may inherit an immortal country. I have read another exposition as if it is Heaven, in which the saints are to dwell, that is indicated by the land of the living ...'[37] He is probably referring to Jerome's remark that specifically denies that the land of the living is the land of Judaea or any other purely terrestrial land, for such are characterized by perplexities and trials; but, rather, the beatitude refers to a better, ideal land, such as the Psalmist yearned for.[38] Similarly, Augustine writes: 'Let the stubborn brawl and contend, then, over earthly and temporal affairs. The meek, however, are blessed because they shall inherit the earth, from which they cannot be expelled ... I believe

---

33. Cf. *Ps* 35(34),10, 'LORD ... thou Saviour of the poor from those too strong for them, the poor and wretched from those who prey on them', also, *Job* 29,12; 36,15; *Ps* 9,18; 10,2 (9,23); 10,9 (9,30); 34,6 (33,7); 40,17 (39,18); 68,9f (67,10f); 70,5 (69,6); 72(71), 2,4,12; 74(73), 19. 21; 86(85), 1f; 109(108), 16,22; *Isa* 3,14; 10,2; 14,52; 26,6; 41,17−20; 58,7; 66,2; *Zech* 7,10; 11,7.

34. *CM* I, on *Mt* 5,3 (*CCSL*, 77, p.24/429−30).

35. Cf. *Ps* 27(26), 13; 52(51), 7; 116(114), 9; 142(141) 5(6); *Isa* 38,11; 53,8; *Jer* 11,19; *Ezek* 26,20; 32,23,24,25,26,27,32.

36. Cf. W.J.P. Boyd, 'Apocalyptic and Life after Death', in *Studia Evangelica* V, ed. F.L. Cross, *T.U.* (1968), Berlin, pp.39ff.

37. *Op. impf. Mt.* Hom. IX, on *Mt* 5,5 (*PG* 56,681.4).

38. *CM* I: *Non terram Iudeae nec terram istius mundi, non terram maledictam spinas et crudelissimus quisque et bellator magis possidet, sed terram quam psalmista desiderat* (*CCSL* 77, p.24/434−7).

it refers to that earth of which it is spoken in the Psalms: "Thou art my hope, my portion in the land of the living" (*Ps* 142,5)'.[39] The *OT*, as interpreted by the Fathers, may well be the source of Aldred's gloss, which reads almost like a paraphrase of *Ps* 37(36),11: 'but the humble shall possess the land'. Certainly he invested *terra* with at least the spiritualized content that the Fathers ascribed to it. However, it may be that he had also read the ***Apocalypse of St Paul***,[40] which has a richly fanciful description of the eschatological *Land of the Meek*:[41] 'And there the land was seven times brighter than silver. And I said: "Lord, what is this place?" and He said unto me: "This is the land of promise. Hast thou not yet heard that which is written: Blessed are the meek, for they shall inherit the earth? The souls of the righteous when they are gone forth out of the body are sent for the time into this place..." '. The seer's *Land* was due to be manifested at the Second Advent. Thus we see a process of development: in the *OT* the land of the living is God's blessing upon the faithful here and now in Canaan. With the Christian doctrine of life after death, it became spiritualized and a symbol of God's kingly rule, sometimes thought of as a realized eschatology in the present, sometimes thought of as life in eternity. In the apocryphal literature, it is a supernatural land belonging entirely to the next world. The ***Apocalypse of Paul*** was one of the basic sources of the ***Divine Comedy*** of Dante.[42] It was written originally in Greek, some time in the third century, and probably in Egypt. Despite an official ban of the Church upon it, a Latin version came into existence in the sixth century. In the late seventh century Aldhelm quotes from it in his work, ***De laudibus virginitatis***, and it was certainly current in England during the tenth century. There is a reference to it in ***The Blickling Homilies***. Ælfric condemns the work as spurious, which is negative testimony to its currency and influence. And Wulfstan refers to the work in his ***Homilies***. There is, therefore, every likelihood that Aldred knew of it, and it may have helped the term *terra viventium* to become a common-place of every-day ecclesiastical speech, thus Symeon of Durham reproduces it in the most natural way in his preface to his ***History of the Church of Durham***, when he implores the general reader of his history to pray for the members of the community of St Cuthbert, so that they might come *videre bona Domini in terra viventium*.[43]

39. *De Sermone Domini in monte libros duos*, I,2.4 (*CCSL* 35, p.4f/82−4). That Augustine's exegesis was widely known is seen in the closeness with which Paschasius Radbertus follows him: see his *Expositio in Matthaeum*, III,5 (*PL* 120,218A−D).

40. T. Silverstein, ed., *Visio Sancti Pauli*, London, 1935.

41. See M.R. James, *The Apocryphal New Testament*, Oxford, 1924, pp.536f for the English translation.

42. Cf. Silverstein, *op. cit.*, p.3.

43. Aldhelm, Bishop of Sherborne (*c.* 640−709). *De laudibus virginitatis: Licet revelatio, quam dicunt pauli, in nave aurea florentis paradisi delicias eundem adisse garriat* (*PL* 89,121D); Blickling Homily IV: Swa Sanctus Paulus cwæþ þætte God hete ealle þa aswæman æt heofona rices dura, þa þe heora cyrican forlætaþ, 7 forhycggaþ þa Godes dreamas to geherenne (R. Morris, ed., *The Blickling Homilies of the Tenth Century*, London, 1874−80, I, p.41). AElfric, *Homilies*, ed. B. Thorpe, London, 1843−6, II, p.332: Humeta rædað sume men ða leasan gesetnysse, ðe hi hatað Paulus gesihðe, nu he sylfe sæde þæt he ða digelan word gehyrde, þe nan eorðlic mann sprecan ne mot? See generally D. Bethurum, ed., *The Homilies of Wulfstan*, Oxford, 1971, pp.278−81, for a discussion of eschatological concepts-in-tenth-century England. For Wulfstan's acquaintance with the *Visio Pauli*, see his Homily 46, ed. A.S. Napier, *Homilien*, Berlin, 1883, I, p.233. Cf. Symeon of Durham, *op. cit.* in n.9 I, p.4.

8 *Mt* 5,6 (34Rb 10ff *rhm*)

esuriunt / hyncgrað (hunger) / eadge biðon ða ðe ðyrstas 7 hyncgras aeft' soðfæstnisse f'ðon ða gefylled biðon in ece líf (Blessed are those that thirst and hunger after righteousness for those will be filled in eternal life).

Aldred appears to be thinking of an eschatological fulfilment of spiritual desire in eternity. By contrast, Augustine apparently interprets this beatitude from the stand-point of realized eschatology, referring to a fulfilment here and now through obedient faith: 'He speaks of those who at this present time love what is true, constant and good. They, therefore, shall be filled with that food of which our Lord himself spoke, "My food is to do the will of my Father" (*J* 4,35), that is righteousness, and with that water of which, whosoever shall drink it, to say the same thing, "it shall be in him a well of water springing up to life eternal" (*J* 4,14; cf. 7,37f)'.[44] However, St Hilary of Poitiers (*c.* 315–67) looks towards a fulfilment of the beatitude in heaven: 'The blessedness which he assigns to those who hunger and thirst after righteousness betokens that the strong, prolonged desire of the saints for the doctrine of God will be sated with good and perfect satisfaction in heaven'.[45] Aldred's interpretation follows this latter tradition, and we may note that once more he prefers an eschatological exegesis. This consistent preference is seen in Glosses 9, 21, 55, and so most probably also in 7 and 8.

9 *Mt* 5,8 (34Rb17ff *rhm*)

corde / of ꝥ fro' hearte (from the heart) / eadge biðon ða clæne hearte bute esuice 7 eghwoelcum facne f'ðon hia geseas god in ecnise (Blessed are the pure in heart, without treachery or any crime, for they shall look on God in eternity).

There is an *OT* context for this beatitude of which Aldred may well have been aware (*Ps* 15(14); 24(23),3f; 51(50),12; 73(72),1). If these Psalms are the source of his comment, it would account for the ethical conditions 'without treachery or any crime'. Aldred here refers to the eschatological concept of the beatific vision, which is entrenched in the Church's teaching about life after death. A classic statement of the doctrine is found in Irenaeus (*c.* 130–2), Bishop of Lyons: 'For the glory of God is a living man, and the life of man is the Vision of God'.[46] In the same passage Irenaeus develops a chain argument for his doctrine of man. First he has to be born, then to grow, then he matures and reaches his full powers. The next stage is to be

---

44. *SDm* 1,2,6, (*CCSL* 35, p.5/93–8).
45. *CM* IV,5 (*PL* 9,932).
46. *Adversus Haereses* IV,20,7 (A. Rousseau, ed., *Irénée de Lyon, Contre les hérésies*, IV, Paris, 1965, pp.648f).

glorified through beholding his Master and Creator, 'For God is the One who shall be seen, and the vision of God creates immortality, and immortality has the effect of making a man near to God'.[47] The Church's teaching about the beatific vision was so universal that it would be impossible to specify a particular source for this gloss. Pseudo-Chrysostom uses *NT* language to express this hope: 'But in that eternal world the pure in heart shall see God face to face, not as now through a mirror and in a riddle as here (1 *Cor* 13,12; and *Mt* 5,8)'.[48] Augustine is concerned to point out that the *OT* assertion that nobody can see the face of God and live does not constitute a denial of the blessed hope of the beatific vision, as these *OT* passages refer to the sight of God through mere bodily senses which would find such a divine disclosure far too overwhelming for their limited capacities.[49] Aldred's expansion of *pure in heart* by *bute esuice 7 eghwoelcum facne* ('without treachery or any crime') reads rather like Jerome's explanation: *Quos non arguit conscientia ulla peccati. Mundus mundo corde conspicitur ...*'.[50]

10 *Mt* 5,9   (34Rb20ff *rhm*)

pacifici / sibsume ł friðgeorne (peaceful or eager for peace) / eadge biðon ða friðgeorne ða ðe hea buta eghwoelcum flita 7 toge behalda(s) ða sint godes sun(a) genemned (blessed are those eager for peace, those who keep themselves without any quarrel or strife they are called the sons of God).

Pacifici can be both active in meaning; 'peace-making', as well as passive, 'of a peaceable disposition'; so Aldred includes both nuances in his gloss. The original Greek word, however, is unequivocally active in meaning: εἰρηνοποιοί 'peace-makers'. Patristic comment tended to include both senses, perhaps inevitably and logically, in that those engaged in reconciliation are likely to prefer to live at peace with their neighbours. Jerome, for instance, has a two-fold qualification of *pacifici* : 'those who first of all are at peace in their own hearts (Aldred's *sibsume*) and thereupon reconcile brothers who are at odds among themselves (*friðgeorne*)'.[51]

11 *Mt* 5,47   (36Vb7 *cm*)

nonne / ahne (ō̄ nonne) / ł sint ða ane ł aron ða ane (either "are the only ones", or "will be the only ones").

Aldred's explanation is obscure as it is unfinished, and it is not clear why he should repeat the comment with a change of verb. Both *sint* and *aron* are plural present

47. *Adversus Haereses* IV, 38.3 (*Ibid*, pp.956f).
48. *Op. impf. Mt* on *Mt* 5,8, (*PG* 56,682).
49. *De Genesi ad litteram* 12.26, (*CSEL* 28,1 pp.418ff).
50. *CM* I on *Mt* 5,8, (*CCSL* 77, p.25/456–8).
51. *CM* I on *Mt* 5,9, (*CCSL* 77, p.25/459–60).

14

indicative forms, but they could also be translated by a future tense in Old English. Perhaps Aldred's comment is part of a line of thought in his own mind, which may have run something like this: 'if they repay only their brethren, do they think that *they are the only ones* (or, *will be the only ones*) who do that kind of thing? Do not even the heathen similarly?'

12 *Mt* 6,24   (30Rb2–5 *rhm*)

mamonae / dioble (devil) / mamon'. Þ is gidsunges hlaferd ðe diowl. he is sua genemned. ma'monis (Mammon's; that is, the lord of avarice, the devil; he is called Mammon).

The usual English spelling, Mammon, is a transliteration of an inferior Greek textual reading, μαμμωνᾶς , derived from the *textus receptus.*   No modern editor of the Greek *NT* text would sanction it, as the Greek uncials and minuscules spell it μαμωνᾶς.   The question of the spelling is important for the etymology of the word, as we shall see below. In the *NT* the word is found four times, only in the sayings of Jesus, and one of these instances is a parallel (*Mt* 6,24 = *L* 16,13; *L* 16,9,11). The Greek word is a transliteration of Aramaic   ממון   , *màmôn,* in its *status emphaticus* form,   ממונא   , *màmônâ* 'wealth', 'property',   and especially 'money'. The word is not found in the Hebrew Bible, though the translators of the *LXX* may have read it in their copy of the Hebrew text of *Ps* 36(37),3 in place of the Massoretic text reading   אמונה   , *'emunah,* 'safe', for instead of the sense 'and find pasture', the *LXX* reads καὶ   ποιμανθήσῃ ἐπὶ τῷ πλούτῳ αὐτῆς, 'and be fed on its wealth'. In the Apocrypha, Sirach has at 31,8: 'Happy is the man who is found blameless And has not erred through pursuing Mammon', where the Hebrew   ממון   is translated in the *LXX* by χρυσίου, 'gold'.

Aramaic *mamon* often occurs in Rabbinic literature with the general sense of 'wealth' or 'riches'.[52] The Aramaic Targums often use the word and it is interesting to see what Biblical Hebrew synonyms attract its use in the Targumic commentary: Hebrew **בצע**   , *betsa',* 'gain', or 'profit', in *Gen* 37,26; *Ex* 18,21 and *Jud* 5,19; **הון**,   *hôn,* 'power', or 'wealth', in *Ps* 44,13(12) and *Prov* 3,9; **כפר**   , *kopher,* 'ransom', or 'redemption price', as in *Ex* 21,30, or 'hush money', as in 1 *Sam* 12,3; or 'bribe', in *Prov* 6,35; **חיל**   , *hayil,* 'wealth', or 'property' as in *Ps* 49,11. These Hebrew equivalents illuminate the ordinary meaning of Aramaic *màmôn.* The Rabbis knew that wealth was perfectly capable of good use, and, as Lightfoot has acutely remarked, wealth rightly used is really almsgiving. But experience showed

52. Cf. for example, the *Mishnah, Pirke ' Aboth*, 2,12: 'Let the riches of thy neighbour be as precious to thee as thy own', which renders: יהי ממון תברך תביב כליך כשלך (P. Blackman, ed., *Mishnayoth,* London, 1951–7, IV, p.503)

15

that the mere possession of wealth, however justifiably gained, tended to militate against the spiritual life, so that even neutral wealth took on a depreciative connotation, which was, of course, strongly explicit for describing dubious or immoral profit, in such Rabbinic phrases as ממון דשקר *mâmôn deshéqer*, 'false mammon'; נזק ממון.ג , *mâmôn nezeq*, 'hurtful mammon'; or ממון אונסיא , *mamon 'ônesayyâ'*, 'mammon of violence', on *Ezek* 22,13; ממון דרשע , *mâmôn deresha'*, 'mammon of wickedness', on *Hab* 2,9; and ממון של גזל , *mâmôn shel gezel*, 'mammon of rapine', on *Isa* 33,15.[53] This emphasis upon the evil effects of mammon naturally led to its personification in the Gospels as elsewhere, through the literary process of metonymy. When we consider Aldred's glosses on *mamonae*, then, we must bear these two aspects of the word in mind: its philological history and its metaphorical usage which developed into an established part of demonology. Scholars are not agreed about the etymology of mammon.[54]

However, a certain measure of agreement has been reached on some matters. It is agreed generally that *mâmôn* is originally Semitic, and that the original spelling has only a single *em* in the middle of the word. This enables the philologist to rule out of court all ingenious suggestions which would require a doubling of the middle *em*, such as the suggestion of W. Gesenius, supported by G. Dalman, that the root is טמן , *t-m-n*, 'to hide', as then we should have to presuppose an original word מטמון *matmôn*, 'treasure', which changes by elision into ממון , *mammon* (our normal English spelling); but such a supposed elision is highly dubious, as an elision of *Teth* and *Mem* in this way would be almost unique. Alternatively, Paul de Lagarde, a scholar of immense authority, suggested the Arabic root *madmun*, equivalent to Aramaic מעמון mâ'môn, 'contents', or 'assets'. F. Delitzsch suggested a derivation from the root מון , *m-w-n*, 'to allot', from which the nouns מנה , *maneh*, 'a coin or measure' of gold or silver (1 *Kg* 10,17; *Ezr* 2,69); or מנה ,

53. Cf. J. Lightfoot, *Horae Hebraicae* III, verse 9, para 2, p.159f.

54. See generally: J. Lightfoot, *Horae Hebraicae et Talmudicae*, revd. ed., G. Gandell, Oxford, 1859, III, pp.159–164; W. Gesenius. *Thesaurus linguae Hebreae et Chaldaeae*, Leipzig, 1829, II, p.552; F. Delitzsch, 'Mammon', *Zeitschrift für die gesammte lutherische Theologie und Kirche*, (1876), 600; P. de Lagarde, *Mitteilungen*, Goettingen, 1884, 226; and *Übersicht über die im Aramäischen, Arabischen, und Hebräischen übliche Bildung der Nomina*, (*Abhandlungen der königlichen Gessellschaft der Wissenschaften zu Göttingen 35*), 1889, p.185; G. Dalman, *Grammatik des jüdisch-palästinischen Aramäisch*, Leipzig, 1894, p.170, n.1; and 'Mammon', *Real-Encyclopädie für protestantische Theologie und Kirche*, ed. A. Hauck, (1898–1908), XII, p.153f; W.H. Bennett, 'Mammon', in *A Dictionary of the Bible*, ed. J. Hastings, Edinburgh, 1900–2, III, p.224; E. Nestle, 'Mammon', in *Encyclopaedia Biblica*, ed. T.K. Cheyne and J.S. Black, London, 1899–1903, III, pp.2912–5; J. Moffatt, 'Mammon', J. Hastings, ed., *A Dictionary of Christ and the Gospels*, Edinburgh, 1906–8, II, p.106g; J.T. Marshall, 'Mammon', J. Hastings, ed., *Encyclopedia of Religion and Ethics*, (1908–26), VIII, p.374f; A.M. Honeyman, 'The Etymology of Mammon', *Archivum Linguisticum*, IV, (1952), p.60–5; F. Hauck,' μαμωνᾶς ', G. Kittel, ed., *Theological Dictionary of the New Testament*, Grand Rapids, Michigan, (1967), IV, p.388; M. Black, *An Aramaic approach to the Gospels and Acts*, 3rd edn., Oxford, 1967, p.139f.

manah, 'portion, part', are derived. He was supported by J. Levy[55] and, more recently, by Honeyman. Most Biblical scholars and Syriacists support the derivation from the root אמן , '-m-n, 'the thing in which men trust', or 'what is entrusted', or 'that which supports and nourishes' the life of man; so, for instance, W.H. Bennett, E. Nestle and F. Hauck *pace* the criticisms of Honeyman. So much for the modern debate.

Jerome knew of the Semitic origin of the word and its meaning. In *Onomastica Sacra* he found the terse rendering Μαμωνᾶ πλοῦτος (*OnS* 183/38); and he expanded that in his *Commentariorum in Mattheum*, 'Mammon — in Syriac speech riches are so termed'. He then pointed out the moral application: 'so let the greedy man who is called by the Christian name take note of this, that he cannot serve both Christ and wealth'.[56] Aldred knew of this linguistic tradition and reproduced it in his gloss on *L* 16,9, mamona / wælo' (riches) ł / .i. sirisc spréc (180Vb23 *rhm*) (i.e. Syrian language).

However, this gloss did not inhibit him from reproducing an alternative marginal comment for both *Mt* 6,24 and *L* 16,11 mamonae /.i. ðæt is diwl gittsung (181Ra8 *cm*) (that is, the devil of avarice, *or* devilish avarice). In these glosses we are faced with the problem of deciding if possible the precise connotation of such words as *dioble, ðe diwl* and *diwl gittsung*. Does Aldred mean the Devil, or merely a devil of avarice, or merely devilish avarice, or all three? Is it *diabolus* or *daemonium* that is intended? It may well be the case that Aldred did not necessarily distinguish between these two connotations, perhaps through the influence of the peculiar character of the demonology of the Gospels, and the Synoptics in particular. In *Mt* 6,24, where Mammon is virtually personified through being placed in parallel with God, the context suggests that Mammon is a symbol for the Devil; though Irenaeus (*Adversus Haereses* III,8) was careful to disallow such a view. Augustine takes it in precisely this way. In his treatise on the Sermon on the Mount, Augustine shows that he is well aware of the normal linguistic meaning of *mammon* through his knowledge of Punic, but that in this Gospel passage the reference is really to the Devil as the alternative master of men: 'Whoever serves mammon justly serves him who presides over earthly affairs, on account of his perversity, whom our Lord described as prince of this world. Therefore a man will either hate this one and love the other, who is God, or he will submit to the one and despise the other. For whoever serves Mammon submits to a hard and destructive Master; for enmeshed by his own avarice, he is subject to the Devil, yet he does not love him, for who is there who loves the Devil?'[57] Augustine's comment was reproduced by Bede and Rabanus Maurus.

55. J. Levy, *Neuhebräisches und chaldäisches Wörterbuch*, 1876–89, III, p.138.
56. *CM* I on *Mt* 6,24, (*CCSL* 77, p.39/828–33).
57. *SDm* II, 14,47, (*CCSL* 35, p.138f/1036–49): *Mammona apud Hebraeos diuitiae appelari dicuntur. Congruit et Punicum nomen; nam lucrum Punice mammon dicitur. Sed qui seruit mammonae* ..... Cf. also Beda, *In Lucam* V on *L* 16,13 (*CCSL* 120, p.299f/154–175) where he combines Jerome's comments with those of Augustine and equates Mammon with *diabolus*; and Hrabanus Maurus, *CM* 2,6 (*PL* 107, 836C–D).

17

However, before we blithely decide that the context must decide the issue, we have to remember that the marginal comments of Aldred are not textual translation but interpretative comment, and therefore it is not irrelevant to look at the way in which he uses these terms elsewhere. He uses *diowl* frequently as a translation for *daemonium* (x 16);[58] *diwles* glosses *daemonia* (x 15);[59] *ðe diwl* glosses *daemonium* at *J* 10,21; *Mt* 17,18 and *Mk* 7,29,30. Then we must remember that one would expect *diabolus* as the Devil to be used absolutely; but the qualification of *diwl* by *gittsung* in *L* 16,11; and of *ðe diwl* by *gidsunges hlaferd* in *Mt* 6,24 suggests that it is one way of recognizing this particular devil or demon, as opposed to, say, a demon of wrath, or a devil of lies (*cf.* 1 *Kg* 22,22). If we allow Aldred a certain flexibility and variation of usage, then it seems not unreasonable to interpret *diwl gittsung* as a metaphorical way of describing a particular vice: 'devilish avarice', which Augustine, as we have seen, reminds us has power to ensnare a man: *sua enim cupiditate inplicatus* (*op.cit.*); but the phrase: *Þ is gidsunges hlaferd ðe diowl, he is sua genemned ma'monis* appears to imply more than a mere vice, rather, a devil responsible for encouraging greed. If so, this may be due to the general influence of the demonology of the Gospels. For, whereas the Devil is referred to eleven times as *diabolus*,[60] (which Aldred glosses by *dioble* x2, *diobul* x3, *diwl* x4) or by a circumlocution such as 'Prince of the devils' in the Synoptics, or its Johannine variant, 'Prince of this world', by contrast the Gospels have many more frequent references to *daemonia*, of which the plural occurs 30 times, the singular *daemonium* x26, *daemones* x5 and *daemon* once.[61] Statistical considerations suggest, then, that either Aldred is thinking of *daemonium* when he uses such words as *diwl* and *dioble* in *Mt* 6,24 and *L* 16,11, or, at least, that such a connotation is not excluded. The problem is not restricted to Aldred, for we find the same kind of comment in the apocryphal *Acts of John*; but once more, when we try to assess any possible connection between this work and Aldred, complex problems of provenance and venue emerge. The *Acts of John* was written originally in Greek, not later than the middle of the second century (*ANT* p.228); the beginning of the Greek text is lost, although extant in a Latin version, and how far this is authentic is not clear. The Latin start

58. *diowl* glosses *daemonium* at *Mt* 12,22; *Mk* 5,15.16.18; *Mt* 9,33; 11,18; 17,18; *Mk* 7,26. 29.30; *L* 7,33; 8,27,29; 9,42; 11,14; 13,32.

59. *diowles* glosses *daemonia* at *Mt* 9,32.34; *Mk* 3,15.22; 6,13; 16,9; *L* 4,41; 8,2.30.35; 9,1; 10,17; 11,15 *bis*; 11.19.

60. *diabolus* occurs at *Mt* 4,1.5.8.11; 13,39; 25,41; *L* 4,2.3.13; 8,12 and *J* 8,44. Note that *diabolus* in *J* 6,70 is metaphorical. The phrase 'Prince of Devils' occurs at *Mt* 9,34; 12,24; *Mk* 3,22; *L* 11,15. The term 'Prince of this world' is exclusively Johannine: *J* 12,31; 13,30; 16,11.

61. *daemonia* occurs at *Mt* 4,24; 8,16.28.33; 9,32; *Mk* 1,32; *Mt* 7,22; 9,34; 10,8; *Mk* 1,39; 3,15; 6,13; 7,26.29.30; 9,38; 16,9; *L* 4,41; 8,2.30.33.35.38; 9,1.49; 10,17; 11,15 *bis*. 18.19.20; *daemonium* occurs at *Mt* 12,22; *Mk* 5,15.16.18; *J* 10,21; *Mt* 9,33; 11,18; 17,18; *Mk* 7,26.29.30; *L* 4,33.35; 7,33; 8,27.29; 9,42; 11,14 *bis*; 13,32; *J* 7,20; 8,48.49.52; 10,20.21; *daemones* occurs at *Mt* 10,8; 12,24; *bis*. 27.28. daemon occurs at *Mt* 9,33.

to the MS runs to about 17 paragraphs before it reaches the point where the Greek text now starts. In paragraph 16 of the Latin version we read: 'For he who loves money is the slave of Mammon, and Mammon is the name of a devil set over carnal gains, and is the master of those enamoured with the world'.[62] The same tradition appears in the *Glossa Ordinaria* on *Mt* 6,24. After quoting Augustine on the impossibility of serving God and the Devil, a note is appended thus: *Et mammonae, Mammona, Syra lingua, divitiae, quibus servire Deum negare est ... Dicitur hoc nomen esse daemonis qui praeest divitiis...* (*PL* 114,105B). When we review the evidence so far presented it seems that it would be possible to regard Augustine as the source of both the apocryphal *Acts of John*'s comment on Mammon, and, perhaps, indirectly, of Aldred's marginal glosses on Mammon, as well as the comment in the *Glossa Ordinaria*, in that all have in common the motif of 'presiding over carnal wealth' as the main function of the demonic role of Mammon. A complicating factor, however, is the testimony of St Paschasius Radbertus who states that Mammon is the name of a devil (i.e. *daemonis*) *qui divitiis praesit hujus saeculi,* (*Exp. in Mt* IV,6,*PL* 120, 307D). We see from this form of the tradition that he has Augustine's key phrase about Mammon's presidency over worldly wealth, but then he goes on to declare that his source is none other than that of Irenaeus himself: *Quod nomen Irenaeus Lugdunensis episcopus et martyr Christi, daemonis esse dicit* (*ibid*). There is a substantial comment on Mammon in *Adversus Haereses* III,8, but nothing corresponding to the statements that we have been discussing. Did Paschasius mix up Augustine and Irenaeus? Or was there another work, possibly attributed to Irenaeus pseudonymously, in which this tradition was located? It is impossible to determine. To sum up, Aldred's glosses on Mammon being the name of a devil that presides over avarice, seem to derive ultimately from Augustine, perhaps as mediated by both apocryphal and late western Church writers. For his linguistic information he is clearly dependent upon Jerome, or those scholars who copied him.

13 *Mt* 6,30 (38Va 17ff *cm*)

uos / iuih (you) / gegerues god suiðor. alle ðingo hæfeð us gesald monnu' bi allu' wihtu' (*deus...uestit...magis.* He has given everything to us men in respect of all things).

Aldred here reproduces typical teaching on Providence in a manner reminiscent of such *NT* passages as 1 *Tim* 6,17: 'God who has given us all things richly to enjoy...' or 1 *Cor* 1,5,7: 'I thank God for all the enrichment that has come to you in Christ ... there is, indeed, no single gift that you lack'.

---

62. J.A. Fabricius, ed., *Codex Apocryphus Novi Testamenti*, Hamburg, 1703, II, p.564.

14 *Mt* 7,6   (39Ra 14ff *rhm*)

s'c'm / halig (holy) / s'c'm cueð halig Þ is ðy halga gesaegdnisse æt hundu' nere gesald Þ is unwyrðu' 7 unclænu ' monnum (s'c'm. He said, 'holy', that is holy sacrifice, should not be given to the dogs, that is to unworthy and impure men).

There are two points of interest here: the interpretation of 'holy' and 'dogs', which for sake of convenience we shall consider in reverse order. The Jews used the term 'dogs', among others, as an abusive epithet for the enemies of Israel: e.g. 1 *Enoch* 89,42: 'And the dogs began to devour those sheep'.[63] This depreciative connotation for dogs was transmitted to the *NT*; so *Phil* 3,2,[64] and *Rev* 22,15.[65] *NT* usage usually interprets 'dogs' in a thoroughly ethical fashion (though *Mt* 15,26 appears to be a notable exception). Aldred inherits this tradition. However, though the original saying has nothing to do with the Eucharist, it soon acquired this connection, and in the early Church the saying was interpreted as an injunction against administering the Holy Communion to the unbaptized. Aldred spells out the tradition by expanding *halig* to *halga gesaegdnisse*,[66] 'holy sacrifice'. Aldred's gloss, then, reflects the tradition concerning the Eucharist which came to be known as the *disciplina arcani* whereby every effort was made to withhold from unbelievers the more sacred doctrines and rites of the Church. In the first place this policy was devised as a practical means of self-defence against persecution and pagan misunderstanding that might give rise to blasphemy or profanation; then, once Christianity became

63. R.H. Charles, ed., *The Apocrypha and Pseudepigrapha of the Old Testament in English,* Oxford, 1913, II, p.254. The dogs are mentioned here in association with foxes and wild boars. The latter were regarded as particularly obnoxious because ritually unclean, quite apart from their ferocity. The association of dogs with swine merely emphasized the depreciatory nuance.

64. βλέπετε τοὺς κύνας,   βλέπετε τοὺς κακοὺς ἐργάτας, βλέπετε τὴν κατανομήν Here dogs are defined by malpractices and those who insist upon what came to be regarded as the mutilation of circumcision.

65. ἔξω οἱ κύνες... The dogs excluded from the new Jerusalem are defined as sorcerers, fornicators, murderers, idolaters and all who practise deceit. It is noticeable that ethnic and religious distinctions have completely given place to moral ones. Thus Aldred gives a *NT* rather than an *OT* interpretation to the term.

66. The *Durham Ritual*, also glossed by Aldred, has *halga asaegdnisso f'e synnum* as the gloss to *sacrificia pro peccatis* (ed. U. Lindelöf, Surtees Society, CXL, 1927, p.88/39). *Saegdnis(s)e, asaegdnis(s)e, gesaegdnis(s)e* is well attested in *Cod.Lind.* in this sense, and *onsaegedness* is recorded elsewhere in Old English. Bosworth and Toller gives as well-attested *onsecgan*, 'to sacrifice' and *onsaegedness*, 'sacrifice', the latter a *-ness* formation to the past participle of the verb (cf. A.S.C. Ross, Aldrediana I Three Suffixes', *Moderna Sprak Language Monographs* 3, 1930, 17). *Secgan* thus has two main meanings: 'say' and 'sacrifice'. J. Pokorny, *Indogermanisches etymologisches Wörterbuch*, pp.897-8 takes both 'say' and 'see' to *seku* of Latin *sequor*, but neither of these well-known etymologies is convincing. There is nothing in *seku* to explain the meaning 'sacrifice'. The two *secgans* are different words; and probably *secgan*, 'to sacrifice' is to the root *sak* – in Latin *sacer, sanctus*; Oscan *sakarater*, 'sacratur'; Hittie *saklai*, 'rite' (Pokorny, *op. cit.* p.878).

accepted by the Roman Imperial state, the tradition settled down into the gradual and progressive enlightenment of the catechumens, to make sure that their faith was built on secure foundations. The earlier symbols of the fish, the lamb and the shepherd were part of this defensive apparatus; its application to the Eucharist was to divide the service into two parts: the mass of the catechumens and the mass of the faithful. The division between these two parts of the service was signalled in earlier times by the orders shouted aloud for the departure of the unbaptized: *Catechumeni recedant. Si quis catechumenus est recedat. Omnes catechumeni exeant foras.* Or *Si quis non communicat, det locum.*[67] This charge of the expulsion of the unbaptized, heretics, or unbelievers was in earlier times regarded as faithful obedience to this particular saying of Jesus: 'Give not that which is holy to the dogs'. The tradition is as early as the second century as the *Didache* testifies.[68] We find it in Jerome in a characteristically original form, for he links *Mt 7,6* with *Mt 15,26* where Jesus says to the woman in Cana: 'It is not right to take the children's bread and throw it to the dogs'.[69] In course of time, as Duchesne explains,[70] the exclusion of catechumens from the Eucharist was no longer practised in the west, largely owing to the almost universal practice of infant baptism, so it was natural for Aldred to interpret 'dogs' in purely ethical rather than ritual terms, as for instance, does Pseudo-Chrysostom in a long discussion of this passage.[71] Yet its connection with the restriction of the Eucharist was too strong to be ignored, so he applies it to the normal pastoral discipline of the Church accepted by all communicant members, that the Eucharist is only for absolved penitents, who have already made their confession as part of their spiritual preparation for the sacrament, and so is not for the impure.

---

67. See L. Duchesne, *Christian Worship, its origin and evolution*, 5th edn., London, 1919, pp.165–75; F.E. Brightman, *Liturgies Eastern and Western*, Oxford, 1896, I, p.462.
68. *Doctrina XII Apostolorum* 9,5:

Μηδεὶς δὲ φαγέτω μηδὲ πιέτω ἀπὸ τῆς εὐχαριστίας ὑμῶν, ἀλλ' οἱ βαπτισθέντες εἰς ὄνομα κυρίου. καὶ γὰρ περὶ τούτου εἴρηκεν ὁ κύριος : Μὴ δῶτε τὸ ἅγιον τοῖς κυσί

(*Mt* 7,6)', (J. Schlecht, ed., *Die Apostellehre in der Liturgie der katholischen Kirche*, Freiburg, 1901, p.114).
69. *CM* I on *Mt* 7,6, (*CCSL* 77, p.42/902–4): *Sanctus panis est filiorum...*
70. *Op. cit.* in n.67, p.171.
71. *Op. impf. Mt hom.* xvii (*PG* 56,727–9, esp. 728): *Propter quod canes puto intelligendos gentiles, vel hæreticos, omino immundos.* Cf. also Paschasius Radbertus: *Nam per canes intelliguntur hi, qui contra veritatem oblatrando impugnant* (*Exp. in Mt* IV, vii in *PL* 120, 317B).

15 *Mt* 7,6 (39Ra 17ff *cm*)

margaritas / meregrotta (pearls) / p'cepta euangelii. Þ aron ða meregrotta Þ sindon godspelles bebodo. ante porcos before bergum ðæt sindon ða mæstelbergas Þ aron ða gehadade menn 7 ða qode menn 7 ða wlonce men f'hogas godes bebod 7 godspelles (p'cepta euangelii. those are the pearls, those are the commandments of the Gospel. ante porcos before swine, those are the fatted swine, those are the men in holy orders and the good men and the proud men. They despise the commandment of God and the Gospel).

One suspects that here we have the exegesis of traditional Gospel symbolism applied to a topical and current situation. As such it will be of the greatest interest for our understanding of Aldred; but first we must see what the traditional exegesis of this passage is, so that we can appreciate the use that Aldred makes of it.

Jerome characterizes the pearl as divine truth that requires faith for its apprehension,[72] and, more particularly, the pearls are the Law and the Prophets. Pseudo-Chrysostom develops the symbolism: the pearls represent 'the mysteries of truth, for as pearls are enclosed in shells in the depths of the sea, so the divine mysteries, enclosed in words, are lodged deep in the unfathomable meaning of the sacred Scriptures'.[73] He may have borrowed some of his ideas here from Isidore's encyclopedia.[74] The context of faith demands an interpretation of swine as unbelievers. Jerome logically explains: 'the swine, then, are those who have not yet believed in the Gospel, and so pass their lives in the bog of unbelief'.[75]

In Aldred's day, of course, unbelief was not so much the problem, and the striking thing about his gloss is his bold application of the saying to clergymen. His gloss appears to be not wholly consistent, for *gode menn* and *wlonce menn* appear to be contradictory. This hiatus may be resolved if we suppose that Aldred applies the term 'good men' to those who are supposed to be good, whose profession is the pursuit of goodness, but who in fact 'despise the commandment of God and his Gospel'. The situation to which Aldred appears to be applying this saying is that of the tenth-century reform of the monastic houses (see the discussion of Glosses 17 – 18 *infra*). Of course, Aldred could answer any possible objectors to his exegesis by saying that he was doing no more than reproduce sound Gospel exegesis sanctioned by the doctors of the Church, for had not Augustine so interpreted the swine who

---

72. *CM* I on *Mt* 7,6: *...cito evangelii credere margaritum*, (*CCSL* 77, p.42/905–13, quotation from 911) and *CM* II, on *Mt* 13,46 (*CCSL* 77, p.113/1025–9; 1025f for quotation): *Bonae margaritae ...lex et prophetae sunt.*

73. *Op. impf. Mt, hom* xvii (*PG* 56, 728–9).

74. Isidorus, Bishop of Spain (560–636), *Etymologiarum sive Originum* I, xx (ed. W.M. Lindsay, Oxford, 1911): *Margarita prima candidarum gemmarum, quam inde margaritum aiunt vocatum quod in conchulis maris hoc genus lapidum inveniatur* (16.10.1).

75. *CM* I on *Mt* 7,6, (*CCSL* 77, p.42/905–13; see 909–11 for quotation).

perished at the healing of the demoniac of Gerasa? (*Mt* 8,28–34 = *Mk* 5,1–20 = *L* 8,26–39). Augustine said of the two thousand swine that rushed headlong over the cliffs into the sea, that they represented 'the impure men and proud men over whom the evil spirits rule on account of their idolatry'. Their violent death in the lake, says Augustine, meant that thereby the Church had been purified.[76] Aldred may have regarded the expulsion of secular clergy from the monasteries in much the same way.

16 *Mt* 8,26 (41Vb 12f *rhm*)

fidei / ðæm ðe tuas ymb godes mæht him f'stondes mæht 7 geleafa f'e is ungelefnise.

The difficulty is to know the meaning of *f'stondes*. It could mean either 'there is available', 'avail', or 'prevail'; so yielding a translation: 'Power and belief will avail (*or* be available to) him (*or* will prevail for him) who doubts about God's power because of his unbelief'. However, such a sentence is self-contradictory. Possibly a *ne* has been missed out between *him* and *f'stondes*. Then it would give good sense: 'Power and belief will *not* avail him who doubts about God's power, because of his unbelief'. Perhaps this marginal comment was hastily written down. Its sentence construction suggests that it was not thought out clearly in advance of its being written. The best method of elucidation appears to be to examine the discussion of the passage in the Fathers and see how Aldred's comment relates to it. It seems that Aldred may have been commenting upon Jerome's exegesis of the miracle of the stilling of the storm. Jerome comments upon the identity of those who were in the boat alongside Jesus, and who were said to have marvelled at the miracle he performed. Jerome observes that the text calls them *homines*, and so adds that they who were so astonished were obviously not disciples, and must have been members of the crew or any others who happened to be in the boat. Then, as if he realised that this piece of exegesis was highly vulnerable to criticism and Jerome could never tolerate criticism of the slightest kind, he immediately adds that if anyone obstinately wished to maintain that the men of little faith who were so astonished were indeed disciples, he would answer that the disciples were rightly described as men who had not yet come to know the power of the Saviour.[77] Aldred's comment fits into this discussion, particularly if seen as his attempt at elucidating when and under what conditions the *potentia Saluatoris* would be available, namely, never to

---

76. *Quaestiones Evangeliorum* II, Q 13, (*PL* 35, 1338).
77. Hieronymus, *CM* I on *Mt* 8,27, (*CCSL* 77, p.52/1188–93) reproduced by Beda, *In Marcum* II, on *Mk* 4,40 and *In Lucam* III, on *L* 8,25 (*CCSL* 120, p.491/75–80, and p.181/611 –14): *Non discipuli sed nautae et ceteri qui in navi erant mirabantur. Sin autem qui contentiose voluerit eos qui mirabantur fuisse discipulos, respondebimus recte homines appellatos, quia necdum potentiam noverant Saluatoris.*

a doubter, as his very doubt would preclude him from the possibility of experiencing that power.

17 *Mt* 10,8   (45Ra upper margin to line 6 *cm*)

gratis date / unboht sellas / Cueð to ðæm apostolum. 7 biscopum æft' him f'ðmest. unboht ge hád fengon 7 unboht ⱡ uˌ ˌceap buta eghuelcum worðe seallás ðæm ðe sie wyrðe ⱡ worð bið in lare 7 in ðæwu' 7 in clænnise 7 in cystum : 7 in lichoma hælo f'ðon bisc' scæl cunnege 7 leornege ðone preost georne buta ær geleornade (He said to the apostles and bishops foremost after him. You received orders gratis; give (them) gratis without any price to those who are worthy in learning and in habits and in purity and in virtues and in health of body. For the bishop must test and teach the priest eagerly, unless he has learnt beforehand).

18 *Mt* 10,14(?)   (45Rb4—8 *rhm*)

et / biscope is f'bod[en] Þ he onfoe niw[e] cumenu' preo[st] 7 to gehælgenne ferunga. leorn[e] hine ærest 7 ge[eorne] gecun^{n}ia 7 ascag[e] ða ðe hine cunn[as] huulic monn sé.....[h] is   lár gesceauig[e] buta he hæbb[e] unf' cúð uitne[sse] [] = *letters trimmed off at the edge.* (A bishop is commanded to receive a newly-arrived priest, and to consecrate him quickly. Let him teach him first and eagerly prove him and ask those who know him what kind of a man he is...(and) examine his doctrine unless he have a good person who will bear witness for him).

Comments 17 and 18 are best taken together, for the remarkable thing about Gloss 18 is that it bears no reference to the text alongside it (hence, presumably, Skeat's ingenious attachment of it to *Et*). It is best taken as a comment additional to Gloss 17. Both glosses raise many points of interest, which are best discussed *seriatim*. (a) 'You received orders gratis, give them gratis, without price to those who are worthy ...'. Aldred applies the original saying of our Lord to the problem of simony in the Church.[78] The term *simony* denotes primarily the practice of the sale or purchase of spiritual grace or functions; then later on it came to be applied to the payment of a consideration for appointment to an ecclesiastical office or living. When the Church was poor and liable to be persecuted, the abuse was comparatively rare; though, of course, it is not unknown in the Scriptures: in the *OT* there is the

---

78. For Simony see generally: A.J. Maclean, 'Simony', *ERE*, 11(1920), 525f; N.A. Weber, *A History of Simony in the Christian Church from the beginning to the death of Charlemagne, 814 A.D.*, Baltimore, 1909; R.A. Ryder, *Simony: An historical synopsis and commentary, 'Catholic University of America Canon Law Studies'*, LXV(1931); A. Bride, 'Simonie', *DTC*, 14, (1941), 2141—60.

case of Gehazi (2 *Kg* 5,20–7), and in the *NT*, Simon Magus (*Ac* 8,18–24) from whose first name the term is derived. When the Church was recognized by the State in the fourth century, the abuse became endemic. R.C. Trench recalls 'the bitter epigram of our English Owen, to the effect that men might dispute whether Peter had ever been at Rome, but none could deny the presence of Simon there', and remarks, 'it was not bitterer than the truth would warrant'.[79] However, the mind of the leaders of the Church was unequivocal: simony was wrong and must be rooted out at all costs. The *Apostolic Canons* (*c.* 400) forbid the giving or receiving of the episcopate, presbyterate or diaconate for money and refer to the deterrent example of Simon Magus.[80] Similarly the second canon of the Council of Chalcedon (451) warns that if a bishop confers ordination in return for money he is liable to be deposed, and those so ordained will lose the dignity or post which they gained by their payment.[81] Though the ban on simony was comprehensive, in that these canons were often copied and included in the decisions of regional synods, the abuse continued to flourish, so that denunciations of simony recur as a frequent feature of the canons of later councils.[82] Of course, a man might have a genuine vocation to holy orders, yet find that he had no option but to pay up for the grace of ordination if he was faced with a firm demand from his bishop, whom he could hardly refuse. At the last session of the Council of Chalcedon Eusebius of Ancyra told his fellow-bishops that his dearest wish was that all ordinations might be free of charge, for he himself had incurred a large debt when he was appointed bishop, a debt which had been first incurred but remained undischarged by his predecessor.[83] We may recall that Aldred tells us in his colophon to the Lindisfarne Gospel codex that he had to pay 'eight ores of silver for his induction', when he joined the community of St Cuthbert at Chester-le-Street.[84] We must not assume that he paid his induction

79. *Lectures on Medieval Church History,* London, 1879, p.339.

80. The Greek text of the Canons was translated into Latin by Dionysius Exiguus (*c.* 500–50), and this is the form in which they were introduced into England by Archbishop Theodore at the Synod of Hertford: *Quibus statim protuli eundem librum canonum...* writes Beda, *HE* IV,5(*op. cit.* in n.3, p.350). Cf. *Canones Apostolorum* xxviii: *Si quis episcopus aut presbiter aut diaconus per pecunias hanc obtenuerit dignitatem, deiciatur et ipse et ordinator eius et a communione modis omnibus abscidatur, sicut Simon magus a me Petro,* (ed. C.H. Turner, *Ecclesiae Occidentalis Monumenta Iuris Antiquissima canonum et conciliorum graecorum interpretationes latinae.* Oxford, 1899, p.20).

81. E. Schwartz, ed., *Concilium Universale Chalcedonense,* Frankfurt, 1936, II, p.106, canon 2: *Siqui episcopus per pecunias ordinationem fecerit et in pretium adduxerit inemptam gratiam et ordinaverit episcopum per pecunias... vel presbyterum vel diaconum ... convictus periclitabitur de suo gradu et qui ordinatur.*

82. Councils which denounce simony are: the second council of Orleans in 533, canons 3,4 (Hefele-LeClercq, II,1133); the sixth council of Toledo in 638, canon 4 (III,280); the eighth council of Toledo in 653, canon 3 (III,290); the eleventh council of Toledo in 675, canon 9 (III,313); the seventh council of Braga in 675, canon 7 (III,314) see also n.89,90 *infra.*

83. Hefele, III, p.427.

84. 7 æht^u ora seolfres (*alt. to seulfres*) mið tó inláde...(259Rb).

fee happily; it may well have been with strong reservations and silent protest. At least he took care to ensure that the Church's explicit and traditional teaching about simony did not go unrecorded when it came to glossing *Mt* 10,8. This was the right place for his remark for this was precisely the Gospel text most used for the Church's denunciation of simony. St Gregory the Great in his letters often used this dominical saying to back up his papal condemnation of the *simoniaca heresis* : 'For from the account given me by certain persons I have learnt that in those parts no one attains to any sacred order without the giving of a consideration. If this is so, I say with tears, I declare with groans, that, when the priestly order has fallen inwardly, neither will it be able to stand long outwardly... For he who is advanced to a sacred order, already tainted in the very root of his promotion, is himself more prepared to sell to others what he has bought. And where is that which is written, "Freely ye have received, freely give" (*Mt* 10,8)? And since the simoniacal heresy was the first to rise against the holy Church, why is it not considered, why is it not seen, that whosoever ordains any one for a price in promoting him causes him to become a heretic'.[85]

It is clear, then, that the colophon and this particular gloss mutually illuminate each other, and when we come to examine the gloss a personal reference cannot be ruled out. In his gloss Aldred spells out the true qualifications for ordination: 'give gratis, without price to those who are worthy in learning and in habits and in purity and in virtues...'. In the colophon he emphasizes that he is worthy in learning and in habits, for he had glossed Matthew for God and St Cuthbert, Mark for the bishop, Luke for the members of the community — which showed concentration and persistence as well as devoted scholarship. As for his virtues, had he not performed a work of supererogation in paying out four more ores of silver for God and St Cuthbert, and had he not glossed St John for the good of his own soul? Yet he was not a proud and arrogant man, for he had a due sense of his own unworthiness before God: 'Aldred a most miserable priest... Aldred a sinner...' were his own self-descriptions.[86] The strong probability that the eight ores of silver represented the price charged for his admission to the community and possibly also to ordination is founded upon the widespread nature of this practice. His gloss addresses itself to the local situation in many monasteries of western Europe during the period of the eighth to the tenth centuries. Owing to the prime need for defence in times of continual hostilities, which in England and elsewhere were occasioned in the ninth century particularly by Scandinavian expansion, rulers often found that the only

---

85. *Registrum Epistolarum,* I, lib. i—viii, ed. P. Ewald and L.M. Hartmann, *Monumenta Germaniae Historica, Epistolae,* Berlin, 1891, V,58, p.369. See also the following letters for a condemnation of simony in conjunction with a quotation of *Mt* 10,8; *Epp.* V,62 (p.377/14); V,63 (p.397/17); VI,7 (p.386/30f); VIII,28 (II, p.29/23—5); IX, 218 (II, p.206/25f).

86. aldrcd peccato' (89Vb), 7 aldred p'sb'r indignus 7 misserrim' (259Rb).

way they could pay for military defence was to appoint leading soldiers as abbots. The result was a decline in monachism and the general secularization of religious houses. A very frank and bitter protest is found in the early-tenth-century council at Trosly in the diocese of Soissons (26th June, 909) : 'Touching the condition, the falling away of monasteries, we scarce know what to say, what to do. For the mass of our crimes and the oncoming judgment from the Lord, our cloisters have been burned and destroyed by the heathen, have been robbed and almost brought to nothing... Monks, canons, nuns, lack their own rightful rulers, are subject, contrary to all law of the Church, to prelates not of their body, and thus are brought to dire need, to sin and confusion ... Now in our monasteries laymen live as lords and masters, presiding over religious life and conversation as though they were professed abbots; their monks give themselves to greed and luxury indecent even for godly layfolk. Nay, more, in consecrated houses of God lay abbots are living with their wives, their sons and their daughters, with their soldiers and their dogs. It is written that abbots shall read, interpret and study their holy Rule with their communities. Who now shall interpret this? Who shall read, who understand? For should you offer these 'abbots' the book of their Rule, they will answer you in the words of Isaiah, "I know not how to read" '.[87] When monasteries were under the control of lay and sometimes illiterate abbots, it was natural and understandable that applications for admission were seen as a lucrative opportunity. The second Council of Nicaea in 787 noted that certain bishops and abbots were in the habit of demanding silver from those who apply for orders or admission to a monastery or convent and denounced the practice.[88] Similarly the Council of Frankfurt in 794 particularly denounced the charging of silver for admission to a religious house.[89] These instances are one and a half centuries earlier than Aldred, yet it seems that nothing had changed in this respect by his day. The abuse, therefore, was widespread and of very long standing. Perhaps it was precisely such facts which lent fuel to the driving force and motivation behind the vigorous reform of religious houses in England which took place in the reign of King Edgar (959–75), when some forty monasteries were either built or restored. Oswald, bishop of Worcester and archbishop of York, and Æthelwold, bishop of Winchester, in particular, expelled many secular clergy from their minsters if they refused to become fully professed monks of the Benedictine order.[90] Now Aldred's Prayer and Colophon to the Lindisfarne Codex betray a

87. Mansi, XVIII, cols 270f.
88. See canon 4 in Mansi, XIII, cols 421–2; Hefele-LeClercq, III,779.
89. Canon 16: *Audivimus quod quidam abbates, cupidate ducti, praemia pro introeuntibus in monasterium requirant. Ideo placuit nobis et sanctae synodo ut pro suscipiendis in sancto ordine fratribus nequaquam pecunia requiratur, sed secundum regulam S. Benedicti suscipiantur* (Hefele-LeClercq, III, 1058).
90. See generally the discussion of the tenth-century reformation in M. Deansley, *The Pre-Conquest Church in England,* London, 1961, pp.276–327; E. John, 'Oswald and the tenth-century reformation', *Journal of Ecclesiastical History,* IX (1958), 159ff.

strong desire for acceptance by the community of St Cuthbert. In all probability he would have been just that kind of candidate who was being encouraged by the Reformers, since his marginal comments on *Mk* 12,25 and *Mt* 1,18, for instance,[91] strongly suggest that he was a celibate and would therefore perhaps be looked upon with some suspicion by the largely secular clerics of the community at Chester-le-Street. We know that the community had undergone a radical change of character since its flight from Lindisfarne in 875 under Abbot Eadred and Bishop Eardulf. For Eadred was the last abbot who was also a monk, until Bishop Ealdhun (990–1018) chose the monk Alfwold as abbot.[92] In fact during their journeyings the members of the Community rarely boasted more than two or three monks, for they never succeeded in making good the loss sustained by the slaughter of monks in the Viking raid on Lindisfarne in 793.[93] Aldred's application for membership, *c.* 960, then, would be considered by a largely secularized community which may have been hesitant and tardy. To have refused this postulant might have resulted in calling undesirable attention to the community's affairs by those ecclesiastical authorities who had the power to change its character radically. To agree would mean that celibate influence and counsels within the community would be increased. Doubtless delay was also occasioned whilst his financial credibility was being established, since the success of his application depended upon his willingness and ability to meet the customary charge. From the outset, however, Aldred had been determined to raise the whole proceedings above the sordid level of a simoniacal transaction; and so as an act of charity and example of virtue, he donated a further four ores of silver for God and St Cuthbert: 7 feouer ora seulfres mið gode 7 sc'i cuðberhtes earnunga (259Rb), to ensure that he was free from complicity in such a transaction, and established his innocence by ensuring that the true teaching of the Church was recorded in his gloss on *Mt* 10,8.

If his application had been subjected to delay and prevarication, it would account for his impatience: 'A bishop is commanded to receive a newly-arrived priest and to consecrate him quickly...'; and that would be very understandable. In general the advice given to bishops by the Church was not to lay hands hastily on any man in ordination.[94] However, Aldred may have considered that in giving such advice he was not making any innovation but merely faithfully following papal advice and precedent, such as when Pope Gregory I counselled a bishop at Palermo about the ordination of a monk to the priesthood, that he should not prevaricate, as there 'ought not to be any delay in answering such a petition ... provided that his life,

---

91. Cf. the discussion of Glosses 4 and 30.
92. Symeon of Durham, *op.cit.* in n.9, I, p.213; E. Craster, *op.cit.* in n.10.
93. E. Craster, *ibid,* 197–8.
94. Cf. Council of Nicaea (325) canon 2 (Hefele-Clark, pp.377–8); Synod of Sardica (*c.*344) canon 3 (Hefele-Oxenham, pp.142–3).

character and actions are worthy of so high an office ...'.[95] Aldred's protest would be against delay for the wrong reasons.

(b) 'For the bishop must test and teach the priest eagerly, unless he has learnt beforehand', and again, 'let him teach him first ...'. Here Aldred emphasizes the teaching office of the bishop, which function has a venerable tradition in the English episcopate. The Chronicle of Æthelweard reminds us that at the Synod of Hatfield in 680 Archbishop Theodore 'strove to communicate divine learning to them'.[96] Alfred the Great (849–99) translated Gregory's *Cura Pastoralis* into English so that the famous treatise on the teaching office of the bishop might edify his subjects, both clerical and lay. In an age when the Church was struggling to recover her learning after it had been swamped by the Danish invasions, this aspect of a bishop's office assumed urgent priority.

(c) 'and eagerly prove him and ask those who know him what kind of man he is ... and examine his doctrine unless he have a good person who will bear witness for him'. An essential part of the process of ordination is the examination of the candidate for orders. A classic example of this requirement is found in the letters of Cyprian of Carthage (*d.* 258). During the Decian persecution he was in hiding, and so had to conduct his diocesan business by letter. With regard to the ordination of Aurelius to the lesser order of Reader, he wrote that he always took into consideration the general advice, *communi consilio*, when weighing the character and merits of individuals.[97] Again, when writing about two lapsed bishops, he observes: 'the priest should be chosen in the presence of the people under the eyes of all, and should be approved worthy and suitable by public judgment and testimony... priestly ordinations ought not to be performed except with the knowledge of the people present, so that in the presence of the people either the crimes of the evil-doers may be revealed or the merits of the good proclaimed, and that the ordination which has been examined by the vote and judgment of all may be just and lawful ... We notice that the apostles observed this, not only in the ordination of bishops and priests but also in the ordination of deacons ... for no unworthy man ought to attain to the ministry of the altar or to priestly rank'.[98] Cyprian's teaching took root in the theory and practice of ordination in the western church as can be seen in the canons of many Church councils.[99] At this point, then, Aldred is witnessing to the time-honoured tradition of the Church.

95. *Registrum Epistolarum* VI, 39 (*MGH Epp.* I, p.415f).
96. A. Campbell, ed., *The Chronicle of Æthelweard,* London, 1962, p.20.
97. *Epistula* 38,1: *In ordinationibus clericis, fratres carissimi, solemus vos ante consulere et mores ac merita singulorum communi consilio ponderare* (*CSEL* III(1868), 579,1/1–2).
98. *Epistula* 67,4, (*CSEL* III, 738/3–739/1).
99. E.g. the Synod of Hippo (393) canon 20: 'No one may be ordained who has not been approved, either by examination or by the testimony of the people' (Hefele, II, p.398). Cf. Concilium Carthaginense (*c.* 398), canon 22: *Ut nullus ordinetur clericus, nisi probatus vel episcoporum examine vel populi testimonio* (Mansi, III,884; and cf., Hefele, II, pp.408f). Cf. further the Council of Clovesho (747), canon 6: *Sexto statutitur decreto: Ut episcopi nullum de clericis seu monachis ad sacrum presbyteri gradum ordinent, nisi prius ejus vitam qualis extiterit, vel tunc morum probitas ac scientia fidei existat, manifeste perquirant: qua namque potest ratione aliis integritatem fidei prædicare, sermonis scientiam conferre, peccantibus discretionem poenitentiæ indicare, nisi prius vigilanti intentione, hæc pro viribus ingenioli sui studeat ediscere* (Haddon and Stubbs, p.364).

(d) 'in health of body'. This phrase recapitulates a requirement of the Church for ordinands that is as old as the Council of Nicaea (325), the first canon of which states that a priest who has undergone surgery with subsequent mutilation may remain among the clergy. If a priest has been disabled by torture at the hands of the barbarians there is no disqualification, 'but if a man in good health has mutilated himself, he must resign his post after the matter has been proved among the clergy, and in future no one who has acted thus should be ordained ...'. As the canon explains, the ban is principally directed against the fanatical asceticism that made some men castrate themselves or undergo such castration as an act of literal obedience to *Mt* 19,12.[100] The idea that a priest should be physically whole and well is derived from *Lev* 21, 16—23: 'No man...who has any physical defect shall come and present the food of his God. No man with a defect shall come, whether a blind man, a lame man, a man stunted or overgrown, a man deformed in foot or hand, or with mis-shapen brows or a film over his eye or a discharge from it, a man who has a scab or eruption or has a testicle ruptured. No descendant of Aaron who has any defect in his body shall approach to present the food-offerings of the LORD ... he may eat the bread of God both from the holy-gifts and from the holiest of holy-gifts, but he shall not come to the veil nor approach the altar, because he has a defect in his body'. We can see immediately how the language of the Nicene canon has been influenced by this Levitical passage; as also that of later Councils.[101] In modern times, of course, with the vast advances in medical skill that have taken place since the fourth century, the requirement of physical health has receded to such an extent that it is rather commonsense than ritual specification which determines whether a physical handicap is a bar to ordination. Aldred would have had every opportunity of being familiar with this traditional requirement, as this particular canon was still being copied as late as 895 when it appears as the 33rd canon of the Council of Thibur.[102] The main reason why the Church endorsed the ancient Jewish requirement was the high view it took of the Eucharist. If what was celebrated was nothing less than the Body and Blood of the Lord, then in order to ensure that his offering

---

100. Canon 1: *De eunuchis. Si quis egritudine faciente a medicis ita forte curetur ut nato in locis vulnere opus sit testiculos amputari aut si cuiquam violenter a barbaris fiat, manest in clero. sin vero sanus aliquis se ipsum absciderit, hunc in clero manere non oportere ac de cetero nullum talium admitti debere. Sicut enim hoc manifestum est abscidentes sese abiciendos esse; ita si quis a barbaris aut a dominis forte castrentur inveniantur autem alio modo digni admittantur ad clerum (op.cit.* in n.81, I, p.112f). Perhaps the best piece of historical gossip is that of Origen's alleged self castration as an illustration of this canon. Although, in his defence, it must be said that there is no evidence that he did so, and substantial arguments can be adduced to show the suspect character of the tradition.

101. E.g. the Council of Rome (465) canon 3 (Hefele-LeClercq II[2],903); also the third Synod of Orleans (538) canon 6: *aut semus corpore, vel qui publice aliquando arreptus est, ad supra-scriptos ordines promoveatur.* In the margin there is: *semus vel senius forte sectus vel servus. semus corpore, id est mutilatus seu murcus'* (Mansi, IX, 13).

102. Mansi, XVIII, 430.

30

was as perfect as possible, the priest must aspire to perfection, not just morally, spiritually and intellectually, but also physically. If the sacrifice had to be perfect then the man who presented it ought to be so also, at least as far as was humanly possible.[103] Aldred's gloss, then, expresses the standard requirement of western canon law.

19 *Mt* 10,16   (45Va1 *Ihm*)

prudentes / hogo (wise) / prudentes in bono. 7 simplices in malo.

Aldred correctly expands the saying: 'Be as wise as serpents and as guileless as doves'.

20 *Mt* 12,8   (49Ra19 *cm*)

sabbati / to sunnadæ ł to seternes dæg (on Sunday or on Saturday) / Þ wæs ðæra iudea sunnadæg (that was the Jews' Sunday).

It is interesting to note how Aldred glosses the occurrences of the word *Sabbath* in the Gospels: *Mt* 12,1 sabbato / in sunnadæg; 12,2 sabbatis / in sunnadagum; 12,5 sabbatis / sunnadagum; sabbatum / sunnadæg; 12,8 is our first example above; 12,10 sabbatis / on sabba'; 12,11 sabbatis / on sabbat'; 12,12 sabbatis / in sabba'; 24,20 sabbato is unglossed; 28/1 sabbati is unglossed; *Mk* 1,21 sabbatis is unglossed; *Mk* 2,23 sabbatis / sunnedagu'; 2,24 sabbatis is unglossed; 2,27 sabbatu' / rest-dæg; sabbatum / ræst dæge; 2,28 sabbati / to ræst daege; 3,2 sabbatis / on haligdagu'; 3,4 sabbatis / hræstdagu'; 6,2 sabbato / haligdoeg ł sunnadoeg; 16,1 sabbatum / ł sunnedaeg; *L* 4,16 sabbati / dæge sun';[104] 4,31 sabbatis / on dagu'; 6,1 in sabbato secundo / on ðone æftíra daeg;6,2 sabbatis / symbel-dagu'; 6,5 sabbati / symbeldæges; 6,6 sabbato / symbeldæge; 6,7 sabbato / symbe'dæg; 6,9 sabbato / on symbeldæg; 13,10 sabbatis / on symbeldagum; 13,14 sabbato / on symbeldagu'; in die sabbati / in dæg symbles; 13,15 sabbato / on symbel-doeg; 14,1 sabbato / on symbel-dæg; 14,3 sabbato / on symbeld'; 14,5 die sabbati / doeg symbol'; 23,54 sabbatum /sunnad'; 23,56 sabbato / sun'; *J* 5,9 sabbatu' / sunnedaeg; 5,10 sabbatum / symbeldæg; 5,16 sabbato / symbeldæg ł ; 5,18 sabbatum / ðone sunnedae; 7,22 sabbato / symb' ł sunned'; 7,23 sabbato / sunnedaege; 9,14 sabbatu' / iud' sunnadæg; 9,16 sabbatum/ sunned'; 19,31 sabbato / on symbeldæg.

---

103. The Anglo-Saxon *Pontificale* of Osmund charges the newly-ordained priest that it will be his solemn duty to 'transform by an unspotted blessing' (*immaculata benedictione transformat*) the bread and the wine offered at Communion into the Body and Blood of the Son of God; D. Rock, *The Church of our Fathers as seen in St Osmund's rite for the Cathedral of Salisbury*, revd. G.W. Hart and W.H. Frere, London, 1905, II, p.24f.

104. A.S.C. Ross, 'Notes on the method of glossing employed in the Lindisfarne Gospels', *Transactions of the Philological Society*, 1933, p.116–7, explains the inverted gloss as arising out of the glossator's desire to preserve the same order of words in his gloss as in the Latin glosseme.

When we look at these glosses we note the very human characteristic of the glossator using the same gloss for a string of instances; then, when there has been a break, using another gloss. The connotations given are (a) holy day, (b) rest day, (c) feast day and (d) Sunday or Saturday. These require further discussion. (a) *holy day*. This gloss for *sabbath* would have been derived from the Scriptures, reinforced by the practice of contemporary Christian worship (cf. *Ex* 16,23 'holy sabbath'; so also *Neh* 9,14; *Jer* 17,22.24.27) and the frequent demands that the sabbath should be made holy (*Ex* 20,8; 31,15; 35,2; *Deut* 5,12; *Ezek* 44,24). (b) *Sabbath as rest day* is explicit in the account of the institution of the sabbath in *Gen* 2,2f: 'and on the seventh day God ceased from all his work. God blessed the seventh day and made it holy, because on that day he ceased from all the work he had set himself to do'. Then phrases such as *sabbath of rest* are very frequent in the *OT* (*Lev* 16,31; 23,3.32; 25,4); also frequent are the prohibitions from working on the sabbath day such as in *Jer* 17,21; 'Bear no burden on the sabbath-day'. (c) *Sabbath as festival day*, or *feast day*, may have come from the Scriptures. In *Lev* 23,2–3 the Sabbath takes pride of place in the Festival calendar (cf. also *Lev* 26,34.43; *Isa* 58,13). Some passages enjoin feast-days with sabbaths (cf. *Lam* 2,6; *Hos* 2,11 and in the *NT, Col* 2,16). More probably Aldred is referring to the common understanding of Sunday in England in his day. In the eighth century, the Council of Clovesho (747) referred to Sunday thus: *De honore et observatione dominici diei...Sed et hoc quoque decernitur quod eo die sive per alias festivitates majores, populus per sacerdotes Dei ad Ecclesiam sæpius invitatus, ad audiendum verbum Dei conveniat. Missarumque sacramentis, ac doctrinæ sermonibus frequentius adsit.*[105] The ecclesiastical code known as *Edgar II*, issued at Andover some time between 959 and 962 and thus contemporaneous with Aldred, ends with the charge: 'Every Sunday shall be kept as a festival from noon on Saturday till dawn on Monday, no work being done.'[106] However, a curious fact about the gloss *symbeldagum* is that it does not occur before *L* 6,2, and Aldred seems to have been very impressed by this meaning for he uses this gloss for the next eleven instances of the word. Now at *L* 6,2 the *Glossa Ordinaria* has *'Sabbata significant feriationes ...' (PL* 114,260). Is this purely coincidence? If not, does this represent early and genuine comment by Walafrid Strabo at this point? If so, this may be the source of Aldred's *symbeldagum*. (d) The gloss *Sunday or on Saturday*, and the marginal comment: 'That was the Jews' Sunday' (cf. the gloss on *J* 9,14; iud' sunnadæg) shows how by Aldred's time *Sabbath* and *Sunday* were regarded as equivalent in the minds of English Christians. I believe that Scottish Presbyterians even today mean 'Sunday' when they use the word 'Sabbath'. For Aldred the two

---

105. Haddan and Stubbs, III, p.367.
106. A.J. Robertson, ed., *The Laws of the Kings of England from Edmund to Henry I*, Cambridge, 1925, pp.22f: 7 healde man aelces Sunnandaeges freolsunga fram Saeternesdaeges nontide ðo Monandaeges lihtinge be þam wite ðe seo domboc taece.

words are obvious synonyms. There is a long and complex historical development behind the pattern of the modern week. At the beginning of the Christian era there were two forms of the week, the Jewish seven-day week which culminated in the Sabbath as its sacred seventh day, and alongside it the planetary week derived from astrology. The names of the individual days of the planetary week were derived from the luminaries of the solar system. The English week substituted the names of Germanic deities for some of the week-day names of the planets. Thus Tiwes dæg (Tuesday) replaced Mars-day (originally ἄρες) etc. The survivals from the planetary week in the English week were Saturn (or χρόνος) hence Saturday; Sun (or ἥλιος) hence Sunday; Moon (or σελήνη) and hence Monday. As the planetary week began with Saturn-day, it followed that Sunday was the second day of the week, but for the Jews it was the first day of their week. Saturday and Sunday tended to become equated as Christians considered Sunday the first day of the week. As Sunday became progressively regarded as the Christian counterpart of the Jewish Sabbath, so it gradually acquired the characteristic of a day of rest. This equation became official after the accession to power of Constantine as Roman emperor. From earliest Christian observance Sunday had been regarded as a festive day, as it was the Feast of the Resurrection, the Lord's Day. However it was also a day when the Christians had to work, for to begin with most of them were slaves and manual workers. In Origen's day he could argue with the Jews that Sunday was superior to the Sabbath because Sunday was *not* a day of rest, as the Sabbath was. The Jews would have agreed that Sunday was a working day, and precisely on that account would not have regarded it as sacred. The sanctity of the Sabbath for them lay in its total prohibition of work from sunset on Friday evening to sunset on the Sabbath. However, Origen inverted the argument. In his *Homilia in Exodum* he argues that the Manna was first given on a Sunday but ceased when the Sabbath dawned, 'so that even then it was made plain that on their sabbath the grace of God would not come down from heaven to them, and the heavenly bread which is the word of God would not come to them'.[107] However, the sun held a special significance for Constantine, as it was the divine portent of Victory for his destiny as a warrior, and closely associated with his conversion to Christianity.[108] Therefore he enacted that Sunday should be a day of rest for everyone, with the possible exception of those engaged in agriculture and farming.[109] Churchmen were quick to endorse the new imperial policy. In the

---

107. *In Exodum Homilia* VII,5: *Quod si ex divinis scripturis hoc constat quod in die dominica Deus pluit manna et in sabbato non pluit, intelligant Iudaei iam tum praelatam esse dominicam nostram Iudaico sabbato, iam tunc indicatum quod in sabbato ipsorum gratia Dei ad eos de coelo nulla descenderit, panis coelestis, qui est sermo Dei, ad eos nullus venerit* (GCS 29, OW 6. p.211/9–14). Of course on Origen's argument every week-day would also have been superior to the sabbath, but wisely he did not press that conclusion.

108. Cf. J. Stevenson, *A New Eusebius; Documents illustrative of the history of the Church to A.D. 337*, London, 1957, pp.299–300.

109. Constantinus, *Corpus Iuris Civilis*, ed. P. Krüger, Berlin, 1954, II, p.127.

Commentary on the Psalms attributed to Eusebius, on the Sabbath Psalm 92 we find: 'Through the new covenant God's Word has, therefore, transferred the sabbath celebration to the light's rising and has given as a type of the true rest, the saving day of the Lord, the first day of light...'[110] Similarly Pseudo-Athanasius can write: 'The Lord has transferred the sabbath day to the Lord's day'.[111]

Aldred may have derived his concept of the equivalence of the Sabbath with the Christian Sunday from his reading of Bede, who in the course of a discussion in which he sought to demonstrate the superiority of the Christian Sunday, only succeeded in emphasizing their counterpart character in his own thinking. Bede explains that on the Sabbath the Jews flocked together in their synagogues to rest from all worldly pursuits, so that they could concentrate with quiet mind on the precepts of the Law. The name *Synagogue* stood not just for the congregation of the faithful, but also for the building in which the Jews gathered to hear the Word of God proclaimed.[112] How suggestive such a discussion would be of the local church in Sunday worship. Aldred's marginal explanation reads like a summary of Bede's discussion.

21 *Mt* 13,30 (53Rb 12 interlinear)

messem / hrípe .i. to domes dæg (harvest, that is to Domesday).

In the Parable of the Tares (*Mt* 13,24–30) Harvest is a clear symbol of the Last Judgement, and the influence of this Gospel parable was strong enough to ensure that it remained such. For example, the Shepherd of Hermas (early second century) relates how the seer beholds the trees in his vision all looking similarly withered, and asks why this should be so. His guide replies that the trees are not all withered, though the live and withered ones look alike; just so, it is not possible to distinguish clearly in this world between the righteous and the sinful. For this world is the wintertime of the righteous, and they are not distinctive in so far as they dwell with sinners; but come the harvest![113] The unity in the point of view with the Parable of the Tares is that judgement is the prerogative of God, who will exercise it in his own good time, so that now is not the time for the expulsion of bad members from the community of the Church. This reminds us that the doctrine of the Last Judgement,

---

110. *PG* 23.1169c.
111. Pseudo-Athanasius, *Hom. de Semente* 1. See the fine discussion by W. Rordorf, *Sunday; the history of the day of rest and worship in the earliest centuries of the Christian Church,* London, 1968.
112. *In Lucam* II, on *L* 4,16 (*CCSL* 120, p.101/56–76).
113. Cf. J.B. Lightfoot, *The Apostolic Fathers,* London, 1926, p.345f for text and translation of Similitude III,2 of the *Shepherd of Hermas.* See also the discussion of the Parable of the Tares in C.H. Dodd, *The Parables of the Kingdom,* London, 1961, pp.137–40; J. Jeremias, *The Parables of Jesus,* 3rd edn., London, 1972, pp.81ff, 224ff; A.W. Argyle, *The Gospel according to Matthew,* Cambridge, 1963, p.105.

for all its fierce apocalyptic imagery, has exercised a beneficent and humane influence upon those religious societies which have subscribed belief in it, since it has acted as a channel for the sublimation of aggressive and censorious attitudes towards others. We find the same theological tendency towards toleration within Islam: the *Murjiites* (*lit.* 'the Postponers') were so called derisively by the much sterner and inflexible *Kharijites*, because the former were less severe in their ethical judgements, and thus less censorious, as a direct result of their view that all judgement was best postponed until the Last Judgement — which view made the Murjiites much more amenable to compromise.

The western Church Fathers were quite clear that the harvest denoted the Last Judgement. So Paschasius Radbertus, summarizing the tradition he had inherited, produces the formula: *Porro quod messis, consummatio saeculi dicitur...sed tunc tempus ejusdem messis erit, id est judicii dies, quando de singulis jubicabitur.*[114] Cf. Remigius: *Messis autem apellatur tempus metendi; per messem vero designatur dies judicii, in quo separandi sunt boni a malis.*[115] Aldred's *domes dæg* is the literal rendering of *dies judicium*, and he may possibly have written this gloss after reading Paschasius or, possibly, Remigius.

22 *Mt* 14,6 (55Rb 16*rhm*)

herodiadis / .i. ðæs cyni'ges broðer láf Þ wæs hire dohter (that is, the widow of the king's brother — that was her daughter).

The relationships within the extended family of Herod the Great, king of the Jews from 40 BC to 4 BC, are notoriously complex, and it is not surprising that the tradition of the Church concerning his family became very confused, or that Aldred has here made a glaring error. In *Mt* 14,3 the Evangelist states that Herod arrested John the Baptist on account of Herodias 'his brother Philip's wife; for John had told him: 'You have no right to her'.' Now if Herodias had been a widow, as Aldred asserts, then John the Baptist would have had no grounds for his moral rebuke; for, indeed, Herod could have claimed that in that case he was a pious Jew fulfilling the Law by marrying her. *Deut* 25,5 states clearly: 'When brothers live together and one of them dies without leaving a son, his widow shall not marry outside the family. Her husband's brother shall have intercourse with her; he shall take her in marriage and do his duty by her as her husband's brother'. The case was very different, however, if the brother was still living, as *Lev* 20,21 makes clear: 'If a man takes his brother's wife, it is impurity. He has brought shame upon his brother; they shall be proscribed'. This enactment reinforces the prohibition of *Lev* 18,16: 'You shall not have intercourse with your brother's wife; that is to bring shame upon him'. Of course, our

---

114. *PL* 120, 495C.
115. *Catena Aurea* I, p.218.

Lord extended the ban to the man who contemplated divorce in the first place in order to be able to remarry, by his logion: 'Whoever divorces his wife and marries another commits adultery against her: so, too, if she divorces her husband and marries another, she commits adultery' (*Mk* 10,11f = *Mt* 19,9; cf. *vv* 3–9). Whether the Baptist shared this latter point of view is an interesting question. Certainly from a Christian ethical standpoint the liaison between Herod and Herodias was doubly irregular, as both had divorced their partners in order to marry each other. Herod had divorced his first wife, daughter of King Aretas IV, as part of a secret pact which he had made with Herodias. Josephus tells us: 'The tetrarch Herod had taken the daughter of Aretas as his wife and had now been married to her for a long time. When starting out for Rome, he lodged with his half-brother Herod, who was born of a different mother, namely the daughter of Simon the high priest. Falling in love with Herodias, the wife of this half-brother – she was a daughter of their brother Aristobulus and sister to Agrippa the Great – he brazenly broached to her the subject of marriage. She accepted and pledged herself to make the transfer to him as soon as he returned from Rome. It was stipulated that he must oust the daughter of Aretas'.[116] There is sharp disagreement between scholars as to whether the Gospel evidence is mistaken about the name of Herodias's first husband. All the MSS of Mark give his name as Philip, but the best texts of *L* 3,19 omit his name. Similarly Codex Bezae (D) and the Latin versions omit the name from the text of *Mt* 14,3. Those scholars who believe the Gospel evidence to be mistaken, suppose that the error arose through the confusion between the name of Herodias's first husband, and the name of the husband of Salome, her daughter; for, shortly after the death of John the Baptist, Salome married her uncle Philip the tetrarch. Interestingly enough, the Gospel evidence has recently received an impressive defence, and it will be intriguing to see what effect it has on further debate.[117] It was Jerome who misled the western Church by identifying Herodias as the daughter of King Aretas.[118] If the learned doctor of the Church could nod in this way, then we may perhaps excuse Aldred for not paying closer attention to the Gospel text.

116. Josephus, *Antiquitates* 18, p.109–10, 'Loeb Classical Library', *Josephus,* ed. L.H. Feldman, London and Harvard, 1965, IX, pp.76–7.

117. See E. Schürer, *The History of the Jewish People in the Age of Jesus Christ,* revd ed. G. Vermes and F. Millar, Edinburgh, 1973. This work denies that Herodias's first husband was named Philip. See also H.W. Hoehner, *Herod Antipas,* Cambridge, 1972, cap. 7 *passim,* where he defends the Gospel without rejecting Josephus's evidence.

118. *CM* II on *Mt* 14,3f: *Vetus narrat historia Philippum Herodis maioris filium, sub quo Dominus fugit in Aegyptum, fratrem huius Herodis, sub quo passus est Christus, duxisse uxorem Herodiadem filiam regis Phetrai, postea vero socerum eius exortis quibusdam contra generum simultatibus, tulisse filiam suam et in dolorem prioris mariti Herodis inimici eius nuptiis copulasse* (*CCSL* 77, 117/1115–21). Cf. Beda, *In Marcum* II on *Mk* 6,17f (*CCSL* 120, 507–8,729–43). The same tradition occurs in Hrabanus Maurus, *CM* V: *Herodiadem, filiam regis Aretae* (*PL* 107, 959B), and in Paschasius Radbertus, *Exp. in Mt* VII: *Herodiadem filiam regis Petiphere.* (*PL* 120, 512C–D).

23 *Mt* 14,26   (56 Va 3ff *lhm*)

est / ða apos' woendon Þte he woere yfel wiht 7 walde hea besuica
(the apostles thought that he was a creature of evil and wanted to
betray them).

The marginal comment really refers to *phantasma,* which Aldred glossed with the
same words, *yfel wiht,* both here and in the parallel passage in *Mk* 6,49. Possibly
the word *phantasma* in late Latin had begun to acquire a depreciative connotation.
Paschasius Radbertus refers to *phantasma* as the sight of that which is against
nature.[119] Aldred's comment appears to be original and not derived from the
Fathers.

24 *Mt* 23,23   (74 Va 8f *lhm*)

menta' et anethum et cyminu' / ðas aron wyrto noma biðon in
lehtunum (these are the names of herbs, they are in gardens).

The Latin translates Greek ' τὸ ἡδύοσμον καὶ τὸ ἄνηθον καὶ τὸ
κύμινον.' of these, τὸ 'ἡδύοσμον (*lit.* 'sweet smelling', from ἡδύς
'sweet' and ὀσμή 'scent') comes to mean 'mint'. τὸ ἄνηθον denotes
'anise' or 'dill'. τὸ κύμινον is the *LXX* transliteration of the Hebrew word
כמן , *kammon,* 'cummin' (cf. *Isa* 28.25.27). In ancient Israel two tithes
were levied: one for the Levites (so *Lev* 27,30): 'Every tithe on land whether from
grain or from the fruit of a tree belongs to the Lord'; and one for the worshipper (so
Dt 14,22f): 'Year by year you shall set aside a tithe of all the produce of your seed,
of everything that grows on the land...'. In later Judaism the tithe was extended to
cover the produce of the vegetable garden. In the Mishna, *Maaser* 1,1 states: 'Everything which is cultivated and may be used for food, and grows out of the earth is
liable for tithe'. *Maaser* 4,5 is more specific: 'Rabbi Eleazar said, "Of dill one must
tithe the seed, and the leaves and the stalks" '.[120] Aldred may have learnt that these
names denoted garden herbs from the parallel passage in Luke: 'You pay tithes of
mint and rue and every garden herb' (*L* 11,42).

25 *Mk* 1,6   (95Vb2 *rhm*)

mel siluestrae / wudu hunig Þ wæxes on wudu bínde (wood honey
that grows in the wood-bine).

Aldred glosses the parallel passage in *Mt* 3,4 thus: *mel siluestre / hunig udu* (wood
honey). It seems likely that Aldred derived his explanation from Pseudo-Jerome's

---

119. *ideo nunc turbantur putantes se·contra naturam ejus videre* (*PL* 120,524D).
120. See P. Blackman, *Mishnayoth,* London; 1951, for a technical description of the plants
mentioned and for the text of quotations.

remark: 'It means that the faithful, inspired by the wild honey, are fed most royally from the untilled wood'.[121]

26 *Mk* 5,9   (103Va 24f *lhm*)

legio / here (army, host) ꝥ xij ðus Þ is legio... wæs diowla legio (or twelve thousand, that is legio; it was a legion of demons).

A Roman legion, when it had its full complement, numbered six thousand soldiers. Aldred would know this from reading Isidore's encyclopedia.[122] Late traditions tended to be rather vague about precise numbers, and obviously from the standpoint of the miracle story the larger the number denoted by *legio* the more miraculous the happening was seen to be. Pseudo-Jerome tells us that a legion numbers ten thousand men.[123] Aldred does not follow Pseudo-Jerome here, perhaps because he had consulted Isidore already. It may be that he was thinking of the Matthaean account of this miracle story where *two* demoniacs are said to be healed (*Mt* 8,28), and so he simply doubled the number on the assumption that there was a legion apiece in each demoniac.

27 *Mk* 6,21   (106Va 10*lhm*)

tribunis / of' ðrím hundradu' tribunus bið f'wost (a tribune is the leader over three hundred).

The Greek word translated by *tribunus* is χιλιάρχος , *chiliarch, lit.* 'leader of a thousand', but this word is used in the *NT* to denote the Roman *tribunus militum*, who normally commanded six hundred men. However, its use in the *NT* is pretty flexible. *J* 18,12 dignifies the commander of the soldiers who arrested Jesus with the title *Chiliarch*, but it has been suggested that he was in all probability little more than a *decurio*, or corporal.[124] By contrast, *Ac* 23,17 distinguishes between a centurion and a chiliarch, for which latter title Schlatter suggested the translation 'colonel'.[125] Certainly the context of *Mk* 6,21 suggests a high ranking officer, for we read that Herod gave a royal banquet for his 'chief officials, commanders and leading men of Galilee'. The source of Aldred's information is not clear.

121. *Commentarius in Evangelium secundum Marcum* I: *et melle silvestri, fideles inspiratis de inculta silva ignibus praeparati ac mergentes significantur* (*PL* 30,593A–B).

122. *Etym.* IX,3.46–7: *Legio sex milium armatorum est... Legio habet sexaginta centurias, manipulos triginta, cohortes duodecim, turmas ducentas.*

123. *CMk* V: *Legio, id est, decem millia* (*PL* 30,606A).

124. P. Winter, 'On the trial of Jesus', *Studia Judaica* I, Berlin, 1961, p.29.

125. A. Schlatter, *Die Apostelgeschichte. Erläuterzungen zum Neuen Testament*, Stuttgart, 1948, *in loc.* I. Haenchen, *The Acts of the Apostles — A Commentary*, Oxford, 1971, p.646, demurs on the grounds that the correspondence between the Roman military ranks and those of modern times is too unequal to permit this kind of easy rendering.

28 *Mk* 8,35 (112Ra 5 *cm*)

eam / hia her on life (it here in Life).

Aldred's terse comment has to be read in close conjunction with the Gospel text, in order to make any sense of it. The first part of the paradoxical saying is, 'Whoever wishes to save his life shall lose it...' which could provoke in the mind of the exegete the additional questions, 'When?' and 'Where?' The exegetical tradition had a choice: on the one hand apocalyptic thought pointed to the Last Judgement as the place and time when final verdicts are delivered and executed; doubtless the saying has often been interpreted in such a way. Alternatively, there was the possibility that man's true life might be lost here and now. St Gregory I, followed by Bede, develop-ing the hint in *J* 12,24 suggested an exegesis on the analogy of sowing seed: *Ac si agricolae dicatur, Frumentum si servas, perdis: si seminas, renovas.*[126] Pseduo-Chrysostom takes a similar line when he says that to die on God's account means eternal life, whereas self-centred life may mean eternal death, which implies that eternal loss may be incurred here and now in this life.[127] If Aldred was taking this kind of interpretation, then his explanation means that the man who seeks to save his life loses it *here in this life*, and not just in the next world.

29 *Mk* 10,25 (115V b17 *rhm*)

camelum / se micla dear (the big animal).

Even if Aldred had never seen a camel, he would know from the Gospel text of this saying that it was a large animal, and patristic comment would endorse this impres-sion. The Latin Fathers followed Jerome, who, of course, would be perfectly familiar with camels from his residence in the Middle East.[128]

---

126. Gregorius I, *Hom. in ev.* (*PL* 76, 1233D) 37B); Beda *In Marcum* II, on *Mk* 8, 33–8 and *L* 9,24 *in Lucam* III (*CCSL* 120, p.539/1993–5; 203/1435f).

127. *Op. impf. in Mt, Hom.* XXVI, 10.39 (*PG* 56,769): *Melius est propter Deum mori, et in perpetuum vivere, quam propter vos vivere et in perpetuum mori. Si ille pro nobis mortuus est, qui mori non poterat, nisi voluisset: quanto magis nos pro eo mori debemus, qui etsi nolumus, mortales sumus.* At least he preserved the paradoxical character of the text he sought to expound.

128. *CM* III on *Mt* 19,24: *Hoc dicto ostenditur non difficile esse sed impossibile. Si enim quomodo camelus non potest intrare per foramen acus, si diues introire non potest in regna caelorum, nullus divitum salvus erit. Sed si legamus Esaiam quomodo cameli Madian et Epha veniant ad Hierusalem cum donis atque muneribus et qui prius curvi erant et vitiorum pravitate distorti ingrediantur portas Hierusalem, videbimus quomodo et isti cameli quibus divites com-parantur* (*CCSL* 77, pp.171f/896–903). Cf. Isidorus, *Ad mysticorum expositiones sacramen-torum, seu quaestiones in Vetus Testamentum seu Quaestiones in Leviticum* (*PL* 83,326) IX.7: *Quid autem sibi vult quod Lex dicit camelum non manducabis? Nisi quod de exemplo animalis vitam damnat informem et criminibus tortuosam?*, and Beda, *In Marcum* III on *Mk* 10,25: *Si facilius est camelum ingentibus membris enormera* (*CCSL* 120, p.561/777–8).

30 *Mk* 12,25 (120Ra bottom of page)

nubentur / gemænsu'ad (united) / .i. ne ceorl hæfis wifes gemana.
ne wif hæfis ceorles on erist ᚻ æft' erest (man will not have intercourse with woman nor woman with man in the resurrection or
after the resurrection).

The gloss suggests that Aldred was a celibate and that he regarded celibacy as the
highest way of life. The form of his remark may have been influenced by Jerome,
who was followed by Bede, when he made the point that nobody would dream of
saying about an inanimate object such as a stone that it neither marries nor is given
in marriage, as that would be absurd, seeing that objects do not possess genital
organs. Therefore, the fact that such a denial could be made about those who will
rise again from the dead implies that because of their resurrection bodies they could
marry and be given in marriage if they so chose; but they do not make this choice
because they have much better things to do; for, adds Bede, they are like the angels
and enjoy the vision of God.[129]

31 *Mk* 12,41 (121Ra17ff *cm*)

gazophilacium / ðæs dores ðe is sua genemned gazophilac' on
hierusal' (the door which is called gazophilac' in Jerusalem).

Jerome tells us that Gaza is a Persian word denoting 'wealth' or 'riches'.[130] We may
recall that he had an excellent library of pagan writers, and doubtless acquired this
information from reading them.[131] Gregory I applied the information which Jerome
gave to the name for the treasury in the temple. Gregory was closely followed by

---

129. Hieronymus, *CM* III, on *Mt* 22,30: *Latina consuetudo graeco idiomati non respondit.
Nubere enim proprie dicuntur mulieres et viri uxores ducere. Sed nos simpliciter dictum intellega-
mus quod nubere de uiris et nubi de uxoribus scriptum sit. Si in resurrectione non nubent neque
nubentur, resurgent ergo corpora quae possunt nubere et nubi. Nemo quippe dicit de lapide et
arbore et his rebus quae non habent membra genitalia, quod non nubant neque nubantur, sed de
his qui cum possint nubere tamen alia ratione non nubunt* (*CCSL* 77, pp.205f/1830–6). Bede
repeats what Jerome says (*CCSL* 120, p.589/1852–62), then adds: *Sunt enim sicut angeli in
caelis qui gloria resurrectionis innouati absque ullo mortis metu absque ulla labe corruptionis
absque ullo terreni status actu perpetua Dei uisione fruuntur* (*ibid,*/1862–5).

130. *Commentariorum in Esaiam libri I–XI* on *Isa* 39,1.2 (*CCSL* 73, p.452/65–6): *Gaza
autem lingua Persarum divitiae nuncupantur. Nec est Hebraeus sermo, sed barbarus.*

131. See, for example, *Pomponii Melae De Chorographia libri tres* (ed. G. Ranstrand, *Studia
Graeca et Latina Gothoburgensia*, 28, 1971, I, 64, p.14/14): *et munita admodum Gaza: sic Persae
aerarium vocant...* or, again, Quintus Curtius, *History of Alexander*, III, xiii.5: *pecuniam regiam-
gazam Persae vocant* (ed. J.C. Rolfe, *Quintus Curtius with an English translation*, London and
Massachusetts, 1946, I, p.146,5.2). Cf. the note in *Thesaurus Linguae Latinae*, VI.2, under *Gaza*,
col.1721; *gazophilacium*, col.1722.

Bede,[132] who further tells us that *gazophilacium* may mean either 'a money-chest' or 'the room where the temple valuables were kept', and suggests that when Jesus is described as teaching in the treasury in *J* 10,23, it was in a room sited close to Solomon's porch. Aldred may have thought that the door from this treasury opened out onto the portico. The vagueness of his gloss suggests that he was no more clear about it than modern *NT* scholars are.[133]

32 *Mk* 14,62   (126Ra 23 *cm*)

uidebitis / 7 gie geseað ł scilon gesea .i. on dom' dæge (you shall see i.e. at Domesday).

Aldred spells out the traditional apocalyptic teaching about the second advent of Christ, which will wind up the historical process and usher in the Blessed Age to come after the Last Judgement. Such an eschatological scheme was constructed out of a certain exegesis of a number of *OT* passages, and is as early as the *NT* itself in origin: in particular, *Ps* 110,1 'The LORD said to my lord, "You shall sit at my right hand, until I make your enemies the footstool under your feet." ' Compare also *Dan* 7,13f 'And I saw one like the son of man coming with the clouds of heaven (quoted in *Mk* 14,62)...sovereignty and glory and kingly power were given to him, so that all people and nations of every language should serve him...'; also *Zech* 12,10, 'but I will pour a spirit of pity and compassion into the line of David... Then shall they look upon me, on him who they have pierced...' (quoted in *Rev* 1,7; cf. *J* 19, 23.37). This apocalyptic tradition is part and parcel of the exegetical tradition of the Church and has never been seriously questioned within the Church until modern times.[134] Bede's comment on *Mk* 14,62 is to invite the Jew, the pagan and heretic to consider how Christ as Son of Man is to sit on the right hand of God the Father and to come in his majesty on the clouds of heaven.[135] Here then, Aldred is reproducing traditional exegesis of this passage.

132. Gregorius I, *Homiliae in Ezechielem* II, *Hom.* VI,2: *Quia sermone Graeco* φυλάττειν *servare dicitur, et gazae lingua Persica divitiae vocantur, gazophylacium locus appellari solet quo divitiae servantur* (*CCSL* 142, p.295/15–17). Cf. Isidorus, *Etym.* xx.9.1: *Gazophylacium arca est ubi colliguntur in templo ea quae ad indigentiam pauperum mittuntur. Compositum est autem nomen de lingua Persa et Graeca, gaza enim linguq Persarum thesaurum,* φυλάκιον *Graece custodia interpretatur.* Bede furnishes an account of the temple treasury in his exegesis *In Marcum* III on *Mk* 12,41 and *In Lucam* V on *L* 21,1 (*CCSL* 120, p.593/2006ff; p.361f/2633–43): *Quia sermone Graeco* φυλάσσειν *servare dicitur et gaza lingua Persicadivitiae vocantur gazophilacium locus appellari solet quo divitiae servantur;* and his exegesis was reproduced by the *Glossa Ordinaria* (*PL* 114,225C).
133. Cf., for example, A. Plummer, *A critical and exegetical commentary on the Gospel according to St Luke,* 4th edn., Edinburgh, 1910, p.475.
134. Cf. C.H. Dodd, *The Apostolic Preaching and its developments,* London, 1963, and his theory of realized eschatology. Dodd's point appears to be that our Lord used apocalyptic imagery and language as a special idiom for the assertion of the vindication of the righteous by a just and merciful God, and that the Church got the message wrong by interpreting it literally.
135. *In Marcum* IV on *Mk* 14,62: *Si ergo tibi in Christo o Iudaee pagane et heretice contemptus infirmitas et crux contumelia est, vide quia per haec filius hominis ad dexteram Dei patris sessurus et ex partu virginis homo natus in sua cum caeli nubibus est maiestate venturus* (*CCSL* 120, p.622/1066–70).

33 *Mk* 14,62   (126Rb1 *rhm*)

uirtutis / ðæs fador' .i. patris (of the Father).

The Matthaean parallel is verbatim (*Mt* 26,64). The Lucan parallel varies the wording thus: *a dextris uirtutis dei* (*L* 22,69); the gloss is an accurate explanation. As we have just seen, *Ps* 110,1 entered deeply into the consciousness of the early Church as a prediction of the resurrection and ascension of Christ. The idiom 'right hand of Power', or, 'right hand of God' is used in various ways. *Eph* 1,20 states the divine resources of power open to the Christian: 'They are measured by God's strength and might which he exerted in Christ when he raised him from the dead, when he enthroned him at his right hand in the heavenly realms, far above all power and dominion, and any title of sovereignty that can be named, not only in this age, but in the age to come'. This is an eloquent and excellent paraphrase of the Markan formula, 'the right hand of Power', (cf. *Col* 3,1; *Heb* 1,3.13; 10,12; 12,2). The *OT* presents as one of the foremost attributes of God his unlimited power; so much so, that the word 'power' is virtually a symbolic name for God. So 1 *Chron* 29,11 'Thine, O Lord is... the power and the glory'; *Job* 26,14 'but the thunder of his power who could fathom?'; *Ps* 147,5 'Mighty is our Lord and great his power...'. Aldred, then, correctly identifies power as a chief attribute of God himself.

34 *Mk* 14,65   (126Rb17)

prophetisa / gewitga .i. hua ðec slog (*a.f.* of slog) (Prophesy i.e. who struck you).

The best MSS for *Mk* have simply 'Prophesy!'; but St Luke adds the question: 'Who is it who struck you?'(*L* 22,64,Προφήτευσον, τίς ἐστιν ὁ παύσας σε;) which in *Cod. Lind.* appears as: *prophetiza quis est te percussit* / gewitga huælc is seðe ðec slog. The Lucan addition makes clear the point of the blind-folding of Jesus, which detail Mark includes but does not explain. Aldred's explanation is derived from the Lucan parallel text.

35 *L* 2,36   (145Ra3 interlinear)

aser / aseres / .i. iacobes sunu (Jacob's son).

Asher, the eighth son of Jacob and the second child by Leah's maid, Zilpah, is mentioned in *Gen* 30,13; 35,26; 46,17; 49,20, and *Ex* 1,4. Aldred would be likely to know this fact from reading the Scriptures, reinforced by his reading such exegesis as that of Bede, who on this verse writes: *Et de tribu Aser, hoc est beati, descendit qui inter patriarchas duodecim ordine nascendi est octauus...* (*In Lucam* I, in *CCSL* 120. p.70/2002–3).

36 *L* 10,33 (167Rb12 interlinear)

samaritanus / samarita' Þ is hæðinmonn (that is a heathen man).

See W.J.P. Boyd, 'Aldrediana VII: Hebraica', *English Philological Studies,* 10 (1967), 26f.

37 *L* 12,6 (171Rb19 *rhm*)

depundio / .i. duo minuta. ꝥ .

We may note here the incorrect reading in the Lindisfarne text, which reads *nonne quinque passeres ueniunt depundio.* Aldred, however, faithfully follows his text and glosses *ueniunt* by *cymeð.* The error is a spelling mistake for *ueneunt,* which renders the original Greek verb πωλοῦνται ,' (they) are sold'. The same error in Latin text with its accompanying Old English gloss recurs in the parallel passage in *Mt* 10, 29: *veniunt/cymas;* but there *depundio* is replaced by *asse.* Bede explains that a *dipondius* is worth two *asses,* so Aldred may have derived his gloss from reading Bede.[136] Doubtless it was his massive respect for the text of the Gospel codex that inhibited Aldred from making corrections to any reading which he knew to be wrong.

38 *L* 12,35 (173Ra4 *cm*)

praecincti / f'egegyrdedo (girt) / .i. mið gódu' dedu' (i.e. with good deeds).

When the Fathers expounded this text, it was usually linked with the following phrase of the text: 'and your lamps burning', though a separate meaning was usually given to each phrase. Gregory I saw the girt loins as a symbol of asceticism. For him the loins were the symbol of male procreative powers, too often abused in sating the lusts of the flesh, so that girt loins denoted sexual continence. Recognizing that this exegesis was perhaps a shade negative, he continues: 'but because it is a small thing not to do evil, unless also men strive to labour in good works, it is added, "And your lamps burning in your hands"; for we hold burning lamps in our hands when by good works we show forth bright examples to our neighbours'.[137] Aldred's comment transfers the exegesis for the burning lamps, then, to the girt loins. Perhaps he felt that psychologically this was truer, for a man is more ready for action if his loins are well girded, and at least he could claim a distinguished precedent for such exegesis in Cyril of Alexandria (Patriarch from 412–44).[138]

136. *In Lucam* IV on *L* 12,6 (*CCSL* 120, p.247/649f, 654–6); cf. Pseudo-Chrysostomus, *Op. impf. in Mt, hom* 25.29 (*PG* 56,764).

137. *Hom. in ev.* I,13 (*PL* 76,1123f). cf. Beda, *In Lucam* IV on 12,35–7 who follows Gregory closely (*CCSL* 120, pp.255f/987–1066).

138. *Explanatio in Lucae Evangelium* (*PG* 72,744 C–D): ἀλλα τὸ τῆς διανοίας ἕτοιμον εἰς φιλεργίαν τὴν ἐφ' ἅπασι δηλονότι τοῖς ἐπαινουμένοις, ὑπεμφήνειεν ἄν τὸ διεζῶσθαι τὴν ὀσφυν.

39 *L* 16,9 (180Vb23 *rhm*)

mamona / wælo' Þ (riches) / .i. sirisc spréc (i.e. Syrian language).

40 *L* 16,11 (181Ra8 *cm*)

mamonae / .i. ðæt is diwl gittsung' (that is, the devil of avarice,
(that is, devilish avarice).

Glosses 39–40 are discussed under Gloss 12, above.

41 *L* 21,9 (192Ra8 *cm*)

seditiones / ymbsetnungo .i. ymb burgu' (seditions, i.e. near the towns).

The parallels in *Mt* 24,6 and *Mk* 13,7 read: πολέμους καὶ ἀκοὰς πολέμων
(wars and rumours of wars), to which Jerome gave varied renderings: *proelia et
opiniones proelium* (*Mt* 24,6) and *bella et opiniones bellorum* (*Mk* 13,7). Luke alone
has instead of 'rumours of wars', the reading ἀκαταστασίας (insurrections),
which Jerome renders by *seditiones.* Aldred's obscure explanation appears to be a
mis-reading of the Latin aphorism of Bede, which he gave twice in his commentaries
on *Mk* 13,7 and *L* 21,9, again allowing for a nice touch of variety in the wording,
suggested by the Latin Gospel text: *Bella ad hostes pertinent seditiones ad ciues* and
Proelia ad hostes pertinent, seditiones ad ciues (*In Marcum* IV and *In Lucam* VI in
CCSL 120, p.596/57–8, and p.365/83–4, respectively). Aldred has mistaken *ciues*
for *ciuitas.* In classical times *ciuitas* occasionally was used in the sense of *urbs* by
meteonymy; but from the fourth century onwards *ciuitas* was a common word for
city or town. Jerome translates the 82 instances of πόλις in the Gospels by
ciuitas in 77 instances; similarly it is Bede's favourite word for town or city. Of the
77 instances in the Latin Gospel text, Aldred glosses them 63 times by *ceastre* and
20 times by *byrig,* the overlap in numbers being accounted for by their use as alternative renderings. Possibly Aldred considered that *ciuitas* still yielded good sense, in
that insurrections are likelier in an urban area than in the depths of the countryside.

42 *L* 23,54 (200Ra11 *cm*)

parasceue / .i. f'egearuung (that is, preparation); cf. *Mt* 27,62
parasceuen / mettes gearwing (preparation of food); *Mk* 15,42 is
unglossed; *J* 19,14 parasceue paschae / metes f'egearuung .i.
p'paratio cibi aer eostro; *J* 19,31 / gearuunga dæge (day of
preparation), and *J* 19,42 (which is Gloss 64 in this study) parasceuen
iudaeoru' / iuðeana gearuung-dæg (Jews' preparation day) / on
ðæm dæge geruadon hiora mett to eastrosymb' (255Vb4 interlinear) (On that day they prepared their food for the Easter feast).

Latin *parasceue* transliterates Greek παρασκευή ({ παρα} σκευάζειν,
'to prepare' for anything, whether it be for war, negotiations, or a visit, or for a meal,

44

as in Herodotus, IX,82.1: Μαρδονίῳ δεῖπνον παρασκευάζειν 'to prepare a dinner for Mardonius', hence 'preparation'. In the **NT** the six occurrences listed above are all conditioned by their reference to the Jewish liturgical calendar. All six have a primary reference to the sixth day of the week, the day before the Sabbath; and so *parasceue,* quite apart from its etymology, is really equivalent to Friday (cf. modern Greek) as the Markan and Lukan references make clear: *Mk* 15, 42' And as it was preparation day (that is, προσάββατον – the day before the Sabbath)'; and *L* 23,54 'It was the day of preparation (NB the **NEB** renders 'It was Friday') and the Sabbath was about to begin'. The importance of *J* 19,14 is that it has the alternative phrase παρασκευῆ τοῦ πάσχα , 'It was the (day of) preparation for the Passover', as this suggests that *parasceue* could also be the day before the major religious festivals. As the Jewish Passover was determined in its dating by reference to the phases of the moon, its date did not necessarily fall on the same day of the week, so the day before the Passover need not theoretically be always Friday. However, as far as the Gospels are concerned, though there may be a difference of dating of the Passover in Holy Week, they are all united in dating the crucifixion to the Friday of that week, now commonly called *Good Friday,* which was by definition *parasceue* for the Sabbath on the following day. There appears to be a divergence of opinion as to the date of Passover in Holy Week. The Synoptics suggest that the Friday was Nisan 15th, the first day of the Passover festival, in which case the Last Supper on the Thursday evening, because it took place after sundown, would have been the Passover meal. The Fourth Gospel, by contrast, seems to have regarded the day following the crucifixion as the Passover as well as Sabbath, in which case Good Friday would have been doubly *parasceue.* To date the Sabbath following Good Friday as the Passover, i.e. Nisan 15th, would have served the theological intentions of the Fourth Evangelist very well, for by this means he was able to present the crucified Christ as the paschal lamb of the Passover celebration par excellence, as he times the crucifixion as beginning at noon on Good Friday (*J* 19,14–16) the very hour at which the paschal lambs were due to be slain on Nisan 14th in preparation for the Passover feast. The marginal comment of Aldred, 'on that day they prepared their food for the Easter feast', is congruous with this practice.

If we enquire into how the term *parasceue* came to denote *Friday,* it appears that *parasceue* by itself is possibly an elliptical form of a longer phrase παρασκευῆ τοῦ σαββάτου , which may represent a Hebrew phrase ערב השבת , *'ereb hashshabbath.* 'eve of the sabbath', or ערב שבת , 'sabbath eve', which would make *parasceue* equivalent to 'eve', i.e. ערב , *'ereb.* It is as if we should speak of the 'Maundy' when we mean 'Maundy Thursday'. The translation *praeparatio*, though etymologically correct, does not really cope with the use of *parasceue* as a temporal phrase denoting a day of the week, but rather it translates

the *content* of Friday, which for a Jew is always filled with preparations of all kinds
to ensure that the Sabbath day is not desecrated in any way. In the Talmud the
sixth day is called ערובתא *'arubhta,* 'evening'.

Aldred derived his connotation of 'preparation' from western Church writers,
who uniformly interpret it in this way.[139]

43 *J* Preface   (204Va21 *rhm*)

interrogantibus quod signum daret soluendi templum / ꝥ ꝥ tacnas
his aganes lichoma erest (or that indicates the resurrection of his
own body).

Aldred correctly identifies the reference in this sentence to *J* 2,19–22: The prefaces
in the Latin Gospel codices usually selected salient features of the Gospel, such as
notable sayings, or miracles which were under discussion in current exegesis. For
exposition of the connection between the destroyed and restored temple and the
passion and resurrection of our Lord there are many useful modern discussions.[140]

44 *J* 1,1   (211 R, in decorated panel)

et uerbum / uord ꝥ is godes sunu (Word, that is, God's Son).

45 *J* 1,14   (211Vb20)

uerbum / uord .i. xs

Glosses 44–5 are best taken together. In his comment Aldred states the Evangelist's
high Christology, which was part of his Logos doctrine. This theological legacy was
absorbed by the early Church, developed by Greek patristic writers, and became
fundamental to Christian understanding of the meaning of Jesus as the divine Son of
God. Aldred would have found such an identification inescapable in the tradition of
the Church. By way of illustration we may cite the Latin commentary on St John
attributed to Bede, which on *J* 1,1 has: *Verbum, id est Filium Dei (PL* 92,539A),
and on 1,14 has: *gratiae plenus et est homo Christus Jesus... (PL* 92.642C; cf. 646C).

139. Cf. Augustinus, *Tr* 117,2: *Parasceue autem latine praeparatio est (CCSL* 36, p.651/4–5);
also Beda, *In Marcum* IV on *Mk* 14,42 (*CCSL* 120, p.637/1635); Isidorus, *De Ecclesiasticis
Officiis* I, xxx (*PL* 83, 764–6).

140. In addition to their relevance for this particular gloss, the following works have proved
particularly useful for the study of all the Johannine glosses: B.F. Westcott, *The Gospel accord-
ing to St John,* London, 1908, I, p.93f; E.C. Hoskyns, *The Fourth Gospel,* London, 1947, p.194f;
C.H. Dodd, *The Interpretation of the Fourth Gospel,* Cambridge, 1953, p.353; and *Historical
Tradition in the Fourth Gospel,* Cambridge, 1963, p.89; C.K. Barrett, *The Gospel according to
St John,* London, 1956, pp.166f; R.H. Lightfoot, *St John's Gospel: A commentary* (ed. C.F.
Evans), Oxford, 1956, pp.112–4; J.N. Sanders, *The Gospel according to St John,* (ed. B.A.
Mastin), London, 1968, pp.118f; R. Bultmann, *The Gospel of John: A Commentary,* Oxford,
1971, pp.122–9; R.E. Brown, *The Gospel according to John,* London, 1971, I, pp.114–
25.

46 *J* 1,16   (212Ra12f *cm*)

gefea (grace) / .i. xs. p. lege ꝉ sp'm s'c'm p' xo æcclesie p' pigno
datum *est.*

The comment refers to *J* 1,17: 'because the law was given by Moses, but grace and
truth came by Jesus Christ'. This verse suggests that there are successive epochs or
dispensations in God's plan of salvation for mankind — a point of view widely held
in the western Church. Basically, there was on the one hand the Old Covenant,
symbolized by the *OT* generally, and especially by the Torah, the hall-mark of Jewry;
on the other hand there was the New Covenant, as expressed in the *NT*, and
especially by the figure of Christ, its founder. Sometimes further distinctions were
added. For instance, Bede interprets the six water-pots in the wedding of Cana
miracle story (cf. *J* 2,6) as symbols of the six ages in the divine plan for world
history: the first was characterized by the slaughter of Abel by Cain; the second was
the Flood; the third is ushered in by the obedience of Abraham in offering up Isaac;
the fourth epoch is the reign of David; the fifth is the time of the exile in Babylon;
and the sixth age was heralded by the Incarnation.[141] Aldred here distinguishes the
period of the historic ministry from the dispensation of the Church inaugurated at
Pentecost by the gift of the Spirit (*Ac* 2). His description of the gift of the Spirit as
the pledge of the Church is derived from the Pauline phrase in 2 *Cor* 5,5: 'God himself has shaped us for this very end; and as a pledge of it he has given the Spirit',
ὁ δοὺς ἡμῖν τὸν ἀρραβῶνα τοῦ Πνεύματος ;   where   ἀρραβών
is reflected in *pignus* of the gloss. Aldred may have been combining the Pauline
phrase with the exegesis in Pseudo-Bede: *Sed pro umbra* (sc. the Law) *lucem
veritatis, pro figura legis ipsam imaginem rerum, quae figurabantur, exhibuit Christus,
quando data Spiritus aperuit discipulis suis sensum...quia dato Spiritus sui dono...*
(*PL* 92, 644D–645A).

47 *J* 2,4   (214Ra4ff *cm*)

tibi / ꝉ huæd gebyreð ðe 7 me to wircanne wundar ær min faeder
uælle of heofnu' gelefa (does it pertain to thee and me to do
miracles before my Father will wish to give permission from heaven).

Aldred's comment may be his attempt to paraphrase the meaning of the text in a
way consonant with patristic exegesis of this verse. The Fathers were concerned to
emphasize that our Lord was not guilty of unfilial rudeness to his mother, but that
none the less he had to emphasize that the plane of miracle belonged to the dimension

---

141. *Hom.. ev.* II, *Hom* I.14 (*CCSL* 122, pp.99–101/134–223); here Bede is dependent upon
Augustine's exposition in his *Tr* IX.6 (*CCSL* 36, pp.93f). C. Plummer believes that Isidore was
Bede's source; (see his *Venerabilis Baedae, Historiam Ecclesiasticam Gentis Anglorum, Historiam Abbatum, Epistolam ad Ecgberctum una cum Historia Abbatum auctore anonymo*, Oxford,
1896, I, p.xli and n.4–6).

of his divinity, whereas his mother could be concerned only with the dimension of his humanity. Thus Augustine says: 'Our Lord Jesus Christ was both God and man. In as much as he was God, he had not a mother... the miracle he was about to do was according to his divine nature, not according to his weakness (i.e. his humanity), as if to say, "That which in me works a miracle was not born of thee"...'.[142] Pseudo-Bede follows Augustine's exegesis of this verse: *quam miraculum erat patrandum, non temporaliter accepisse de matre, sed per æternitatem semper habuisse de Patre* (*PL* 92,657C). Aldred reproduces this theme freely in his own words, as far as we can tell.

48 *J* 2,6   (214Ra15 *cm*)

singuli /syndrige (each one) / ꝥ eghuælc an uæs tui sestre gemet uel ꝥ ðrea fullunga (each one was exactly a two or three-sester measure).

The gloss seems to be confused. Did Aldred mean that each pot was a two-sester measure but by no means, say, a two-and-a-half-sester, or slightly more than three-sester measure? If so, then it is an absurd remark, without significance. However, the source of this gloss arose from a misunderstanding of Augustine's comment: 'But what means this, "They contained two or three measures apiece?" This phrase certainly conveys to us a mysterious meaning. For by *metretae* he means certain measures, as if he should say, "jars, flasks", or something similar. *Metreta* is the name of a measure and takes its name from the word 'measure'. For μέτρον is the Greek word for measure, whence the word *metretae* is derived: They contained, therefore, two or three metretae apiece'.[143] Aldred seems to have regarded the phrase 'certain measures' as 'exact measures', *mensuras quasdam*.

49 *J* 3,20   (216Ra24 and b1)

lucem / leht .i. xs (bis) (Light, that is Christ).

The Gospel prologue (*J* 1,1−14) emphasizes the character of the Logos as light (see verses 4−5, 8−9). We saw from Gloss 45 that Aldred accurately equates *Logos*, or 'Word' with Christ. The equation is a commonplace of Johannine and subsequent theological thought, as for example in the writings of Augustine.[144]

---

142. *Tr* VIII,9 (*CCSL* 36, p.87/2−13); cf. Beda, *Homelia* I,14 (*CCSL* 122, p.97/71f, 76−82).
143. *Tr* IX,7 (*CCSL* 36, p.94/1−7).
144. Cf. *Tr* XII.13: *ut uenirent ad lucem, id est, ad Christum* (*CCSL* 36, p.128/9); *Tr* XII,14: *lucet dies, Christus est dies* (p.129/5f); *Tr* XIII,5: *Quam lucem ? 'In principio erat Verbum et Verbum erat apud Deum'* (p.132/20f).

50 J 3,23 (216Rb15)

salim ðær stoue æt ðæm uætru' (*a.f.* uætre) (at Salim, the place
by the waters (*a.f.* water).

Cf. the text of this verse: 'Salim because there was much water there'. Jerome has
the note: *Salim pugilli siue uolae aut ortus aquarum, quod breuius graece dicitur*
βρύοντα   (*OnS* 66,19). Aldred's gloss simply reflects the Gospel text he was
glossing.

51 J 5,2 (220Ra2 *lhm*)

bethsaida / bethesda

Any Greek **NT** with a good critical apparatus will show the widely variant spellings
of the place-name: βηϑζαϑά   **א**,   33 (*it.* Betzata);   βηζαϑά
L it^e; Betzetha it^b ff^2;   βελζεϑά   D it^a;   βηϑσαϊδά   (*J* 1,44) 0125.
it^aur,c; Vg. Syr. Copt. Tert. Jerome;   βηϑεσδά   A C K X Δ Θ π 063 078 f^1 f^13
28 565 700 892 1009 1010 1071 1079 1195 1216 1230 1241 ℓ242 etc.   Aldred
shows that he is familiar with this widely attested variant. This gloss, then, is another
example of his practice of following or consulting a manuscript with a different
textual tradition from that of *Cod. Lind.*[145]

52 J 7,38 (228Ra20)

aquae uiuae / uætro cuico ɫ lifigiendo laro (living waters or living
doctrines).

There is a fine discussion of this verse in R.E. Brown (I,390—9). Aldred reproduces
a traditional symbol of living water, which is as old as the Wisdom literature. *Prov*
18,4 has: 'the words of a man's mouth are a gushing torrent, but deep is the water
in the well of Wisdom'. The contrast made here is with foolish speech: 'for when the
fool talks, contention follows' (18,6). Similarly, *Ecclus* 24,30 has: 'I will pour out
doctrine like prophecy, and bequeath it to future generations'. Aldred's reading of
such verses may have been supplemented by Gregory I's remark: 'When sacred preaching flows from the mouth of the faithful, it is as if rivers of living water run down
from the bellies of believers'.[146]

---

145. For further examples of different textual traditions followed by Aldred see A.S.C. Ross,
'The errors in the Old English Gloss to the Lindisfarne Gospels', *Review of English Studies,*
8 (1932).

146. *Homiliae in Hiezechielem Prophetam* I, hom.X,6 (*CCSL* 142, p.147/83—5).

53 *J* 12,6 (239Rb 21 *rhm*)

habens ea / hæfde ðailca penicas (*a.f.* pendicas) (he had that money).

Aldred appears to be commenting on the text which refers to Judas's dishonest administration of the disciples' cash reserves (12,6; 13,29).

54 *J* 13,24 (243Ra13)

petrus / petrus .i. cephas

Aldred would know of the equivalence of these names from the Gospel text of *J* 1,42 *uocaueris cephas quod interpretatur petrus*; or from reading Bede: *Idem ergo Graece siue Latine Petrus quod Syriace Cephas...*[147]

55 *J* 16,23 (248Va21)

in nomine meo / on ðæm lætmeste dæg (on the last day)

At first sight there appears to be little connection between the gloss and its underlying Latin, which is glossed correctly in the *cm* : *in minum noma* (in my name). The gloss reiterates the sense of the opening phrase of the verse, *et in illo die,* which in the *OT* is a well-known eschatological *terminus technicus*, a short-hand way of referring to the fuller phrase, 'the Day of the Lord' Heb: (Cf. *Am* 5,18.20; 8,3.9.11; *Isa* 2,11.12.17.20; *Zeph* 1,7.8.9.10.14.15.16.18; 2,2.3 etc.). יום יהוה

The question poses itself as to why Aldred should have written his gloss over the words *in nomine meo* instead of over *et in illo die*? It seems to me to be highly probable that he was copying Pseudo-Bede at this point, for *Ps-Bede* at *J* 16,23 writes: *In illo die in nomine meo petetis. In futuro enim saeculo cum pervenerimus ad regnum, ubi similes ei erimus, quoniam videbimus eum sicuti est* (1*J*3,2)..... (*PL* 92,865C). Aldred, then, can link 'in my name' with 'in that day', i.e. on the last day, because this link has already been made for him in the commentary he is following.

56 *J* 18,12 (251Rb1)

cohors / Þ compuearod roemisce ł fíf húnd cempo (the Roman body of fighting men or five hundred warriors) / ðreat turma .i. xxxii equites tuu 7 ðrittih eorodmonn (251Rb15f *rhm*): (troop.... thirty-two cavalry men).

Latin *cohors* renders Greek σπεῖρα , which occurs seven times in the *NT* (*Mt* 27,27; *Mk* 15,16; *J* 18,3.12; *Ac* 10,1; 21,31; 27,1). It is a technical term for a unit in

147. *In Marcum* I, on *Mk* 3,16 (*CCSL* 120, p.470/1320) also *In Lucam* II on *L* 6,14 (p.133/1281,1291f). It was certainly an exegetical commonplace of course owing to the prominence of Peter as the chief apostle: cf. Augustinus, *Cons.ev.* II,17.34 (*CSEL* 43,pp.134—5).

the Roman army. Aldred has reproduced Isidore's note: *Cohors quingentos milites habet* (*Etym*, IX,iii.52). It seems as if the marginal comment is an after-thought, since it occurs half-way down the page and is quite detached from the first gloss. On the composition of a *turma*, Isidore has: *Turma triginta equites sunt* (*ibid*, IX, iii.51). The discrepancy in the numbers shows that Aldred's text was late, for W. Smith, the Latin lexicographer, tells us that though the *turma* consisted originally of thirty cavalry, later on it comprised thirty-two riders. Was Aldred's edition of Isidore altered to conform with the later number? Or did he derive this from another source?

Of course there is no suggestion at all of cavalry having been used in the arrest of Jesus in any Gospel narrative. The position of Aldred's comment on the page of the codex suggests that he may have been recording a datum of educational information for its own interest, rather than trying to expound the text at this point. We see here an example of that sharp curiosity which led him to make the educational additions to the *Durham Ritual*.[148]

57 *J* 19,13   (253Vb14 interlinear)

lithostrotus / .i. *est* lapide stratus

See W.J.P. Boyd, 'Aldrediana VII: Hebraica', *English Philological Studies*, 10 (1967), 7ff.

58 *J* 19,25   (254Vb1)

cleopae / cle' .i.*est* uif ⱦ moder (wife or mother).

The equivocal Greek phrase is Μαρία ἡ τοῦ Κλωπᾶ the interpretation of which is neatly side-stepped by Jerome who rendered it: *Maria Cleopae*, for grammatically Clopas could be either a brother, father or son of Mary, if we take Clopas as a masculine name, as the case of the definite article suggests we should. Clopas is usually taken as such and is regarded as the Semitic form of the Greek counterpart *Cleopas* in *L* 24,18, where once more it is presumed by the use of the masculine article that a male disciple is designated. Aldred offers us at least two out of the three possibilities.

59 *J* 19,30   (255Ra2ff *cm*)

consummatum est / gifyllid is. ⱦ. geendad is (it is ended) / .i. Þ uitgadóm 7 allra canone cuido ða ðe ymb crist' ðroung acueden wæs ⱦ weron (the prophecy and the sayings of all the canons which were said about Christ's passion).

Aldred seems to have found it difficult to distinguish between the meanings of 'to complete' or 'to fulfil' on the one hand, and 'to end' on the other. He may have

148. Cf. F. Wormald, 'Aldred's Educational Additions', in T.J. Brown, *op. cit.* in n. 11, p.51f.

been loosely reproducing Augustine's comment: *Consummatum est, Quid, nisi quod prophetia tanto ante praedixerat?*[149]

60 *J* 19,36   (255Rb14 *cm*)

scribtura / in exodo

The *OT* references are *Ex* 12,46; *Nu* 9,12; the reference in *Ps* 34,20, although bearing the same words, has a different meaning. Aldred correctly identifies the source of the quotation. He may have been helped by Augustine's clue, when he comments on the passage: '...an injunction laid upon those who were commanded to celebrate the passover by the sacrifice of a sheep in the old law, which went before as a shadow of the passion of Christ'.[150]

61 *J* 19,37   (255R b18 *cm*)

scribtura / in zacharia

The reference is *Zech* 12,10 repeated at *Rev* 1,7. Aldred correctly identifies the *OT* quotation. He may have been helped by Jerome's remark in his preface to Genesis, where he cites various *OT* texts at random and challenges his critics to identify their sources. If they find this task too difficult, then he, Jerome, will be happy to oblige. The third quotation in his collection of puzzling texts is *Videbunt in quem conpunxerunt*, which he proceeds to identify: *tertium in Zaccharia...*[151]

62 *J* 19,38   (255Rb19f *rhm*)

post / .i. *est* in die examinis iudicii. districti iudicis. ðus beda ðe bróema bóecere cuæð (thus said Bede, the famous scribe).

It has proved impossible to pin down the precise reference in Bede. Aldred may have derived his explanation from Bede's *Explanatio Apocalypsis*, in which Bede on *Rev* 1,7 writes: *In eadem illum forma videntes judicem potentem, in qua velut minimum judicaverunt, sera semetipsos poenitentia lamentabunt.*[152] The greatest value of this marginal explanation is that Aldred confirms Bede as one of the sources of his scholarship.

63 *J* 19,39   (255Va13f)

murrae / ðara wyrtana of tuæ ' treu' recelcs (incense of the herbs from two trees).

Aldred may have derived his comment from reading the Scriptures. *Num* 24,6 speaks

149. *Tr* CIX,6 (*CCSL* 36, p.660/2−3).
150. *Tr* CXX,3 (*CCSL* 36, p.662/14−6).
151. *Incipit prologus in Pentateucho* (in the critical edition of *Biblia Sacra iuxta Vulgatam versionem,* ed. B. Fischer *et. al.*, Stuttgart, 1975,I, p.3).
152. *Explanatio Apocalypsis* on *Rev* 1,7 (*PL* 93,135A).

of aloe trees; and the *Song of Songs* 4,31 more especially has: 'Your two cheeks are an orchard of pomegranates, an orchard full of rare fruits: spikenard and saffron, sweet-cane and cinnamon with every incense-bearing tree myrrh and aloes with all choicest spices'. Aldred may have consulted Isidore's paragraphs *De Aromaticis Arboribus*, in his encyclopedia: *Myrra arbor Arabiae altitudinis quinque cubitorum, similis spinae quam* ἄκανθον *dicunt: cuius gutta viridis atque amara; unde et nomen accepit myrra. Gutta eius sponte manans pretiosior est, elicita corticis vulnere vilior iudicatur. Sarmentis eius Arabes ignes fovent, quorum fumo satis noxio, nisi ad odorem storacis occurrant, plerumque insanabiles morbos contrahunt.*[153]

64 *J* 19,42 (255Vb4)

parasceuen iudaeoru' / on ðæm dæge geruadon hiora mett to eastrosymb'.

See Gloss 42 above.

65 *J* 20,2 (255Vb17)

discipulum / ðegne / .i. ioh' filius zebe'

The Gospel text here refers to 'the disciple whom Jesus loved' (cf. *J* 13,23–6; 19, 25–7; 21,7.20–3.24). The identity of the beloved disciple has been very widely discussed in modern times. However, the tradition of the Church is quite firm and unvarying in identifying him with the Apostle John, the brother of James and son of Zebedee. This John is said to have died as a very old man in Ephesus. The tradition goes as far back as Irenaeus: 'Then John the disciple who had leaned also against his breast, himself also gave out the Gospel when he was living at Ephesus in Asia.[154] By the first quarter of the third century this equation had become conventional in the western Church, through being incorporated by Jerome in the Vulgate preface to the Gospel according to St John. Aldred would be powerfully reminded of the tradition when he came to gloss the preface to the fourth Gospel (202V): *Ioannes euangelista unus ex discipulis dei ... et huic matrem sua' iens ad crucem commendauit* (cf. *J* 19,26). The evidence of the Gospel preface would be confirmed by reading such western Fathers as Augustine, who on *J* 13,21–6, says: 'Now there was leaning on Jesus' breast one of the disciples whom Jesus loved... it was the same John as the one whose Gospel is before us, as he afterwards explicitly says...'[155] It would have been remarkable, then, if Aldred had made any other identification than John the Son of Zebedee as the Beloved Disciple. However, in modern times the traditional

---

153. *Etym.,* XVII,8,4.
154. *Adversus Haereses* III,1,2 (*op. cit.* in n.46, p.34.96).
155. *Tr* LXI, 4 (*CCSL* 36, p.481/1–4); cf. *Tr* CXXIV, 1 (p.680/2–3) and *Tr* XVI,2 (p.165/19 –22).

position has been strongly assailed as well as resolutely defended, so that some Johanine scholars are quite agnostic about the whole issue of both the identity of the Beloved Disciple as well as the authorship of the Gospel.[156]

66 *J* 20,12 (256Rb19f)

angelos / engles (angels) / .i. tuoege erendureco of heofnum cᵁomun (i.e. two messengers came from heaven).

Augustine raises the query whether those who are called *nuntii* really refer to those beings who in Greek are called ἄγγελοι .[157] He did not seem to realize that the Greek word is a direct translation equivalent of the Latin, and is capable like the Latin word of either a secular or supernatural meaning. Aldred, however, shows that he is quite clear that the messengers came from heaven and were angelic beings.

67 *J* 20,16 (256Va21 *cm*)

maria / mar' (Mary) / Þis on englis hlafdia (that is in English, lady).

Cf. the discussion of this gloss in W.J.P. Boyd, 'Aldrediana VII: Hebraica', *English Philological Studies,* 10 (1967), 18–20. This particular connotation emerged especially in the patristic discussion of *Gal* 4,4. Cf. Origenes, *In Leviticum, hom.* 8. 1–2 in *GCS* 29, *OW* 6, p.395/8–11: *Maria 'mulier' in scripturis nominatur – sic enim dicit Apostolus...* The fusion of this exegesis with the etymology of *domina* for *Maria* led to the honorific English title 'Our Lady' for the Virgin Mary. Here Aldred does not notice that the Mary in question is, in fact, Mary Magdalene and not the Virgin Mary.

68 *J* 20,16 (256Va23)

rabboni / .i. bonus doctor

Rabbi is a late Jewish word not prefixed to the name of any teacher before AD 70. Its literal meaning is 'my great one' (= 'lord, master'). In *J* 1,38 we have the Evangelist's (or an editorial) interpretation: 'Rabbi, which means a teacher'. This usage is supported by early ossuary evidence that the Greek word διδάσκαλος was used as a title.[158] This fact suggests the equation διδάσκαλος = רבי , *rabbi.* The form of the word in *J* 20, 16 is Aramaic רבבוני , *rabboni,* 'My master'. W.F. Albright argues that the form is a diminutive of affection or caritative of *Rabbi*

---

156. Cf. Sanders-Mastin, (*op. cit.* in n.140), pp.32–44, for a powerful, critical examination of the earliest evidence, and R.E. Brown, I, lxxxvii-xcii, for a well-argued defence of the traditional position.

157. *Tr* CXXI, (*CCSL* 36, p.66ff/27–8) repeated in Pseudo-Bede on *J* 20,12 *PL* 92,918D): '*Quid est quod unus ad caput, et ad pedes alter sedebat? An, quoniam qui graece angeli dicuntur, latine sunt nuntii?*'

158. Cf. E.L. Sukenik, *Jüdische Gräber Jerusalem um Christi Geburt,* Jerusalem, 1931, pp.17f.

with the meaning 'my (dear *or* little) master'.[159] Professor Loewe dissents from this view and informs me that the diminutive interpretation is by no means certain, and that powerful arguments to the contrary could be made. Though the word means 'Master', its usual *NT* connotation may have been 'teacher'; so *J* 3,2: 'Rabbi, we know you are a teacher sent by God...'. Aldred, aware of its double connotation of 'master' and 'teacher', may have derived his adjective from *Mt* 19,16 *magister bone*.

69 *J* 20,24   (257Ra 20 *cm*)

didymus / in cregesc (in Greek) / geminus in lætin (in Latin)

Aldred may have learnt that didymus was a transliteration of a Greek word from reading Bede or Jerome: ***Thomas abyssus uel geminus, quod est Graece Didimus.***[160] We know that Aldred could not read Greek, and so this datum of linguistic knowledge is derived from those who could.

70 *J* 21,15 (258Val top margin)

prandissent / gihriordadon (dined)/ ða hiæ him uerun gifæ (when they had been given to him).

This comment clearly cannot possibly refer to the breakfast as Skeat's placing suggests, but surely must refer to the dominical charge, 'Feed my lambs'. Aldred's marginal comment is the commonsense observation that the charge could not be carried out before that time when St Peter assumed pastoral oversight of the Church.

71 *J* 21,16   (258Va14 *cm*)

agnos meos / lamboro mino (my lambs) / ðæt arun ða soðfæsta menn (those are the righteous men).

Aldred makes a logical deduction, as 'flock' is a common metaphor for the community of the faithful: cf. *L* 12,32; *Ac* 20,28f; 1 *Pe* 5,2; also God is often symbolized by the figure of the Shepherd: *Ps* 23,1; 80,1; *Isa* 40,11; 44,28; whilst Christ is called the Good Shepherd in *J* 10,2.11.14.16; *Heb* 13,20; 1 *Pe* 2,25; 5,4. Aldred may have also recalled the dominical charge to the Seventy in *L* 10,3; *Ite ecce ego mitto uos sicut agnos inter lupos*.

159. W.F. Albright, 'Recent discoveries in Palestine and the Gospel of St John', in W.D. Davies and D. Daube, ed., *The background of the New Testament and its eschatology*, Cambridge, 1964, p.158.
160. Cf. Beda *In Marcum* I in *CCSL* 120 p.472/1369; Jerome, *OnS* 72/6 *CCSL* 72 p.135/20–1).

CONCLUSIONS

Aldred's glosses to the Lindisfarne Gospels reveal him as a Catholic Churchman, an ascetic and a diligent scribe, who faithfully transmitted the Gospel exegetical tradition of the Church as he had received it from the writings of Jerome, Augustine, Gregory I, Isidore, Bede and those later western writers more or less contemporary with himself. He was well-read in the Scriptures, of which he made intelligent use. His vocation as a Benedictine monk gave him a taste for those apocryphal works in which the ascetic philosophy, that virginity is the noblest way of life, was fitly expressed. In only two glosses do personal considerations perhaps obtrude themselves; but then only as a personal experience of the widespread abuse of simony which was wholly contrary to the ethos of the very Gospel which he was glossing. His work reveals a high sense of responsibility and dedication to his task. As a scribe working in the scriptorium of the Church of St Cuthbert in Chester-le-Street in the last half of the tenth century, during the happy reign of King Edgar, Aldred is a worthy example of English scholarship struggling up out of the ignorance imposed by the ninth-century havoc wrought by the Danes. Edgar's reign, building on the sound work of his predecessors, enabled the Church to recover from disruption and put its house in order. A most urgent task for the Church was not merely preserving and multiplying its precious store of manuscripts, but also communicating divine learning to the faithful. And this meant that Latin texts had to be rendered into the vernacular which, despite its regional dialects, was showing remarkable vitality and suitability as a vehicle for divine learning. Aldred's work as a glossator stands as a substantial monument to this period of the language's development.

If we try to be more specific about his library, we labour under the great difficulty that he rarely cites his sources, with the result that we gain only an *impression* of what works he had at his disposal. The study of Aldred's glosses strongly suggests that he had access to Jerome's *Liber interpretationis hebraicorum nominum* and his main biblical commentaries, *Commentarii in Esaiam, in Ezechielem, in Euangelium*

Matthaei, in iv epistulas Paulinas (ad Galatas, ad Ephesios, ad Titum, ad Philonem), his homilies, and also, possibly, his correspondence. He appears to have relied upon pseudonymous works attributed to Jerome, such as *Interpretatio alphabeti Hebraeorum* and *Commentarius in Euangelium secundum Marcum.* He appears to have been familiar with Augustine's exegetical works on the Gospels, such as *De sermone Domini in monte, Tractatus in Euangelium Ioannis* and his *De consensu Euangelistarum.* He appears to have consulted Isidore's encyclopedia, *Etymologiarum sive Originum* and may have known his *De ortu et obitu Patrum.* The works of Gregory the Great appear to have been available to him, particularly his *Moralia sive Expositio in Iob,* his *Homiliae in Ezechielem, Homiliae in Euangelia* and his *Registrum epistularum.* He appears to have read Pseudo-Chrysostom's *Opus imperfectum in Matthaeum.* Above all he had the scholarship of Bede to fall back upon (cf. Gloss 62). He may have read his *OT* expositions such as *In Samuelem prophetam allegorica expositio, In Esdram et Nehemiam prophetas allegorica expositio, In librum patris Tobiae allegorica expositio,*[161] as well as his famous Gospel commentaries, *In Marcum et in Lucam expositio.* He seems to have consulted his *Super Acta Apostolorum expositio* as well as his *Explanatio Apocalypsis.* His comments on the Gospels are often best illustrated by Bede's *Homeliarum euangelii libri ii.*

The *familia* of St Cuthbert was well-pleased with his work, and under the episcopate of Bishop Ælfsige, Aldred became Provost by 970. He was relied upon sufficiently by his bishop to be chosen to accompany him together with King Kenneth, a minor Scottish monarch, when the latter went to the court of King Edgar to affirm his loyalty to his West-Saxon overlord. That was the occasion when Aldred took the opportunity of entering four collects in honour of St Cuthbert in the Durham Ritual, a book of prayers for a priest which he both greatly expanded and glossed. The additions which he made to that book exemplify the educational needs of the new members of the community. By that time the reforms of Dunstan were working well, and had imparted a new vigour to religious houses such as that of Chester-le-Street. One cannot study Aldred's glosses without acquiring a deep respect for his scholarship at a time when all scholars laboured under considerable handicaps. Despite all his linguistic inadequacies, he none the less succeeded in grasping the main thrust of the Church's exegetical tradition and so faithfully reproduces astonishingly accurate interpretations.

161. Cf. W.J.P. Boyd, 'Aldrediana xxv: *Ritual* Hebraica', *English Philological Studies,* 14(1975), 1–57.

INDEX OF SCRIPTURAL PASSAGES CITED

Abbreviations of Biblical books:

Gen = Genesis; *Ex* = Exodus; *Lev* = Leviticus; *Num* = Numbers; *Dt* or *Deut* = Deuteronomy; *Jos* = Joshua; *Jud* = Judges; 1 & 2 *Sam* = Samuel; 1 & 2 *Kg* = Kings; 1 & 2 *Chron* = Chronicles; *Ezr* = Ezra; *Neh* = Nehemiah; *Ps* = Psalms; *Prov* or *Prv* = Proverbs; *S of S* = Song of Songs; *Isa* = Isaiah; *Jer* = Jeremiah; *Lam* = Lamentations; *Ez* or *Ezek* = Ezekiel; *Dan* = Daniel; *Hos* = Hosea; *Am* = Amos; *Hab* = Habakkuk; *Zeph* = Zephaniah; *Hag* = Haggai; *Zech* = Zechariah; *Wisd* = Wisdom; *Ecclus* or *Sir* = Ecclesiasticus or the Wisdom of Jesus son of Sirach; *Mt* = Matthew; *Mk* = Mark; *L* = Luke; *J* = John; *Ac* = Acts of the Apostles; *Rom* = Romans; 1 & 2 *Cor* = Corinthians; *Gal* = Galatians; *Eph* = Ephesians; *Phil* = Philippians; *Col* = Colossians; 1 *Tim* = Timothy; *Heb* = Hebrews; 1 & 2 *Pe* = Peter; 1 *J* = John; *Rev* or *Apoc* = the Revelation or Apocalypse of St John.